MW01600769

# A Different Drummer

by

K.D. Richardson

II

To Smitty: True friendship lasts a lifetime.

# Chapter 1

## A Sour Note

*"And I don't want the world to see me,*

*'cause I don't think that they'd understand,*

*When everything's made to be broken,*

*I just want you to know who I am."*

~ John Rzeznik- Goo Goo Dolls' *Iris*

He was born Ross Taylor. Early in his music career, he flipped his first and last names and became Taylor Ross. He thought it would advance his career. As you will find, it must have worked.

To my way of thinking, the word 'legacy' is reserved for those who make a significant positive difference while on this plane. Such was the case with Taylor. He was one of those individuals, rare as they may be, that crosses our paths and leaves behind a prominent footprint upon our souls. It's been said that as a man acquires wisdom, he can positively change his life. The truly wise man can change ours in the process.

Throughout life, certain people are called to do certain things, and Taylor answered the call. Now, I wouldn't say that he was the greatest or most important man who ever lived. He was, however, the most interesting individual I ever met.

Upon most people's passing, a headstone is placed to mark the final resting place of that individual, and on it is recorded a beginning and ending date. In between the two is a hyphen. That small dash represents the most important part of a soul's existence, for it's what happens between the opening and closing of a person's life that typically defines their character.

'Once upon a time' wouldn't do Taylor's life justice. Actually, his story didn't take place that long ago.

***

I grew up with Ross Taylor, as he was known back then. We attended the same Ohio schools from kindergarten until he eventually dropped out after our junior year in high school. It was the sixties, and there was a lot of that going on. Some left the academic world to enlist in the army—to assist in the military conflict in Southeast Asia—while others fled the area to avoid the same fracas. I served, and things worked out well for me afterwards when I utilized my G.I. Bill and eventually found employment in the business offices at the local paper mill. I retired after getting my twenty-five years in. I had to. My wife was ill and needed me. Taylor, as some would argue, went on to bigger and better things.

As I mentioned earlier, Taylor left high school in late 1967. He heard about the great happenings going on out in San Francisco, so he hitched a ride out to the Bay area the day after school ended and engaged in the whole hippie thing during the so-called 'Summer of Love.' He frequented the traditional hip gathering sites like Haight-Ashbury, Winterland, and so on.

It was just after the fourth day of July during that year when Vincent 'Vinnie' Vaughn, a well-known experimental drummer in the area, introduced Taylor to John Winston, a guitarist who led the daily pick-up band in the park. His group was performing an outdoor impromptu concert one night, and that was the norm rather than the exception. While Taylor didn't play with John's band that evening, he joined the small audience and took it all in. He became hooked on the music, the crowds, and the whole performing atmosphere. Afterwards, he asked Winston if he could sit in with the band at their next practice; John agreed, and things rolled from there.

When the whole 'Summer of Love' thing started, it was all very cool, as Taylor put it—but this little peaceful happening grew like wildfire, and before long, there were thousands and thousands of people in the Haight-Ashbury neighborhood and the surrounding vicinity. Despite the compassionate efforts of the sympathetic do-gooders, services for the masses became exceedingly stretched. Taylor and the boys quickly realized that if they wanted to survive, they would have to sing for their supper, as the old adage goes. In this case, that saying was right on the money. They were eventually able to land a few weekend gigs at some of the area gathering places, and that provided them with enough money to eat on during the week. They stayed at one of the many flop-houses for shelter, and practiced in the park during the day. What else did they have to do? Through it all, Taylor said that never once did he ask himself, "What in the hell am I doing out here?"

Anyway, it was at one of those weekenders, on October 7, 1967—specifically, at a dive called Rudy's—where they got their big break. They were spotted by a promoter and asked to join Pink Floyd and Sopwith Camel in a benefit later that month at the Fillmore for radio station KPFA, and needless to say they were beside themselves. It didn't get any bigger than that. The rest, as they say, is history.

Actually, that isn't too far from the truth, in their case. Their counter-culture band, Vulture, wowed the radio audience that evening, and was signed within the week to a record deal. Over the next nineteen years, they went on to sell something like seventy-five million albums in the US alone. That's comparable to groups such as KISS or Van Halen in their prime. That, mind you, was when the listening audience was a bit smaller, and when they still made albums.

During their formative days, Taylor 'Rocks,' as he came to be known by his fans during his playing days, along with Ernie 'Red' Huber, John Winston, or J-Dub as they called him, Pete 'Pops' Dixon, and 'Clueless' Joe Paxton were referred to as street pickers by some of the regulars out in the Bay Area. The group accepted that idiom, and after a combination music and pot-smoking session, settled on the name The Screaching Vultures for their group. No one really liked it, so they shortened it to just Vulture, it stuck, and it made them all millionaires.

Flash ahead some thirty-five years, and Taylor found himself living alone in a massive Franklin Canyon concrete-and-marble mansion just outside Hollywood, California. That locale suited him. It was a quiet, calm, lonely area, and in the midst of the life he once lived, Taylor desperately needed some tranquility within his soul. He never did anything half way, though.

Contributing to the serenity of Franklin Canyon was the absence of nearby industry, traffic was at an absolute minimum, and it was close enough to the rat race, yet far enough for his daily escape. Taylor was especially drawn to this particular home site because the reservoir, located just a mile north of his estate, was used for the exterior while filming the opening of *The Andy Griffith Show* back in the early 1960s.

Taylor loved to hike down there regularly and was practically hypnotized by the sound of the gravel crunching under his feet during his nightly visits. He'd sit on a bench at the water's edge and just listen for the crickets. When their pitch began to noticeably increase, Taylor knew it was time to leave, for darkness wasn't far behind. When he rose from the bench, he'd skip a rock across 'Myers Lake,' just like Opie did during the opening of the famous TV show.

As he aged, Taylor's visits became less frequent. Perhaps he ultimately came to the conclusion that places such as the Mayberrys of this world are merely a figment of a writer's imagination. To be honest, this fantasy was probably no different than the mythical people Taylor sang about in his songs—but maybe he finally saw through the haze of his life and realized that a Shangri-La just doesn't exist in this plane. It's also possible that his increased use of recreational drugs was to blame for the sporadic visits and limited physical activity.

You see, as a boy, young Taylor dreamed of an idyllic existence in a town like Mayberry. It could have been Mayberry, Mayfair, New Rochelle, or any other fictional media-born town he was familiar with, because those places were in direct contrast to what Taylor had to deal with at home. His real life was anything but ideal.

Taylor essentially grew up without a mother. Oh, she was around, but flighty, to put it mildly. Even though she was a housewife, she was rarely home. She slept around on her husband for years before the two decided to put an end to their marital charade. Remember, this was a time when divorce was still relatively uncommon and looked down upon. That marital betrayal took its toll on the elder Taylor—and he took it out on his son. Lenny Taylor took to the bottle with added frequency as the years passed as well, and for the most part, Ross Taylor was on his own as he entered his teen years.

Getting back to Taylor and his mansion in the hills of Beverly, by the time the early 2000s rolled around, it had been well over a decade and a half since he'd performed with Vulture. The members didn't see eye-to-eye on anything anymore. On top of that, Taylor rarely made any public appearances. He'd become a bit of a hermit and spent his days watching TV, smoking dope, and taking solitary walks along the paths of the canyon while questioning the meaning

5

of life. Taylor had his groceries delivered, and on rare occasions, his agent would drop off some clothing, dope, or other daily necessities. He had to show something for the retainer Taylor paid him. Such was the life of this aging rock legend.

It was on a Tuesday in the fall of 2004 that everything changed. While it was a typical early October day for most involved, Taylor's life, my life, and the lives of many of the people who lived in Hamilton would transform from the usual to the exceptional. It was the beginning to a magical year.

As per his standard, Taylor was still asleep as the clock neared the noon hour. Despite my harsh description of him and his circumstances, Taylor kept a fairly neat homestead. He was proud of that place that he had worked so hard to afford. The hallway leading to the bedroom was lined with gold and platinum records from years gone by, and while he didn't overdo the publicity photo décor thing– at least in the upper floor of this palatial mansion–he certainly had plenty of press-worthy memorabilia to use if he so chose. It was Taylor's desire to have those who visited know who he was and where he came from, but at the same time he didn't want to dwell on that fact.

I'm not sure what time Taylor would have gotten out of bed if it hadn't been for the ringing of the telephone, but that was more than enough to break the silence in his secluded home. After the fourth ring, Taylor's heavy hand looped over and hit the speaker phone on the end table.

"Yeah?"

"Taylor, my man, how's it hanging?" It was Jerry Langdon, Taylor's often-absent agent.

"Jerry, what the hell do you want?"

"Aw, come on, Tay, I come bearing tidings of great joy."

"Yeah, right. What kind of crapola do you have for me today? And speaking of which, where the hell have you been? You only show up when you want something. So what do you need today, leech?"

"Is that any way to greet the agent who's about to make you a bundle of money?"

"I have a bundle of money, Jer. Cash I don't need. Give me peace of mind and maybe a little smoke, and you have a deal."

"Then how about a gig? I have the ultimate planned for you. Get this–a reunion tour. All of the biggest bands are pulling off this retro crap. People want to hear the old music, you stumble through twenty cities, a live album will be made simultaneously, and voila! You're back in the saddle."

Taylor righted himself in bed. "I don't want to get back in the saddle. Hell, I'm too old to tour, Jer."

"Don't hand me that crap. Mick and the boys are doing it, and Aerosmith's still going strong. I got you that week-long gig on Letterman six months ago. You were superb."

"Yeah, that was the last time I heard from you."

"That's the nature of the business, you know that. We can be friends, but we're co-workers first."

"That's *when* you work. I'm out of the business, Jer. Plus, I haven't seen any of the other guys for years. You know the last time we were together we did nothing but argue. I think I ended that session by telling all of them to go to hell. Bunch of egotists. I was really hacked, so much so that I didn't even attend John's funeral.

Perhaps I should have, but I didn't. I'm done with them, man. It just wouldn't work."

"Don't hand me that! You're just pissed that the Eagles beat you to the punch. You never did like Henley. Look, the way I see it, we can get a fill-in studio musician for John, or perhaps a big-name looking for a gig, add a back-up rhythm section—"

"Then you can get a fill-in for me as well. Even if I didn't hate those guys, at this point in my life, my nerves are shot, my hands are all arthritic, and my hearing's about gone. Hell, I'm over fifty years old. I've had my last hurrah, Jer."

Jerry wasn't about to give up. "Come on, man, put aside your differences. Look at it this way; it would be a great way to keep your name out there."

"It would be a great way for us to earn you a pot of money. What, did you blow all of your dough at the book in Vegas again? I don't care about keeping my name out there anymore. I'm done, man. I'm officially retired, Jer. Beat it."

Taylor reached over and clicked the phone off. He sat on the edge of the bed for a spell, then ran his hands through his long, thin graying hair. He stood, steadied himself, and then gathered up a handful of prescription drug bottles from the dresser top before stumbling his way towards the bathroom.

Once he was as awake as he planned to be for the day, Taylor threw on a pair of jogging shorts, grabbed a bottle of orange juice from the refrigerator and retired to the patio. He sat for a while, but not too long, as he finished his orange juice. He scooted his ashtray and aluminum box over, removed and lit up a marijuana joint, then proceeded to inhale the weed until it was too stubby to bother with. Taylor discarded the butt into a sand bucket near his feet. He prided himself on the fact that his economic stature allowed him to partake in his vice in this manner. Unlike the common man, he didn't have to worry about saving the roaches for a desperation smoke.

After that session, Taylor just stared out over the valley for an inordinate amount of time at nothing in particular before determining that it was too warm to continue. He gathered himself up and returned to the living room. He plopped on the couch, picked up the remote, and turned on the TV. He surfed through the channels, not really caring whether something grabbed his interest or not. After completing a cycle through the available channels, he turned the TV off and once again stared out the picture window. Taylor was drifting through his usual daily funk when the phone on the end table rang. That ordinarily would have caused the average man to startle, but Taylor's buzz kept that reflex in check for the most part.

"Leave me alone!" His shout echoed off the walls of the empty house. Despite his wish to remain isolated, he picked up the receiver and found it was his doctor's office calling.

"Yes, Taylor, this is Dr. Reinhardt's office. You were absent for your scheduled eleven AM appointment this morning. We're going to have to charge you for this."

"Ask me if I care."

"I beg your pardon?"

"I said that I really don't give a shit at this point."

"Sir, please watch your language. When would you like to be rescheduled?"

"How about when hell freezes over."

"What?"

"You heard what I said. Go to hell. I'm done with you people."

Taylor clicked off the phone, then launched it across the room, striking a drinking glass that had been sitting on the half-wall separating the kitchen from the living room. The glass tumbled into the sink and disassembled. He sat on the couch for a moment, his head resting against his palm. Then, as if inspired, he reached over to the end table and opened his cell phone. He dialed Information.

"Yes...um...do you have a number for a Dave or Davis Smith in Hamilton, Ohio? After a few moments, he said, "Hold on, hold on, let me get...", then realizing he was speaking to a recording, he snarled, "Yes, repeat, you dumb-ass," as he hit the numeral 'one' on his phone, then listened again. He jotted down the number, then hung up.

Taylor took another moment to stare out towards the valley, this gaze longer than the last. Then, as if resigned to his fate, he opened his cell phone and once again dialed. After a three rings, there was an answer.

"Davis Smith, please. Oh, this is Dave? The big D! How the hell are you, guy? What do you mean, who is this? It's me, Taylor Ross...uh, I mean Ross Taylor. Yeah, how about that? Yes, it has been a long time, something like thirty-five years or so. Wow, man, that is a long time. Yeah, it's been way too long. Sorry I haven't kept in touch, dude, but...yeah, touring did take up a lot of my time, but that's in the past."

Straightening up a bit in his chair, Taylor continued. "How have you been? A grandfather? You're kidding? I thought you had to become a father first." There was a pause. "I see. I'll be damned. It has been a long time. I guess I missed a lot," he said while wiping his face with his hand from his forehead to his chin.

"Why am I calling? Well, I thought I'd head back to the old stomping grounds this upcoming week. Yeah, it's been a long time since I've ventured back that way. Anyway, I thought if you were still in the area, perhaps we could get together. Yeah, that would really be far out. Oh cool. When? How about Wed...no wait, make it Friday. I'll grab the earliest flight out and get there around noonish or so. Oh, that sounds great. I'm looking forward to it. I'll let you know when my flight gets in. Great. Good to hear your voice again, Smitty. You take care of yourself. Catch you later."

Taylor hanged up the phone and said, "Oh Lordy...what have I done?"

True to his word, Taylor got back to me and we set a time for me to pick him up. His plane got in around one o'clock that afternoon, and I was there waiting on him. I wasn't sure what to expect as I hadn't seen him in person since we were teenagers. The stills I viewed from his concert days didn't do him justice–plus they were a couple of decades old.

The only person who could match my old friend's description entered the terminal shouldering a bag. My God, it was him. His hair was still hippie-length, he sported a grey-stubbled beard, if you wanted to call it that, and his once full face was now hollow and a bit on the gaunt side. He reminded me of a shorter, skinnier version of Lenny Taylor when I had last seen him, but Taylor looked even more haggard than he had. I was shocked, to say the least, but I wasn't surprised.

"Good God, Taylor, how are you doing? Man, you're a ..."

"A mess? Probably. Yeah, I don't get out too often these days. Wow, look at you. You're an old man now."

"Me? Don't tell me you don't have a mirror out there in L.A."

11

"Well, perhaps I have changed a little bit. Wow, I haven't been to Cincinnati since we did a tour stop back in the early eighties. I think it was one of the first bookings for the Coliseum after those eleven kids were trampled to death at The Who concert."

"Yeah I know. I was at your concert that night."

"Oh wow, man, why didn't you tell me? I could have comped you a couple of free tickets, backstage passes, and everything. Hell, I could have had you sitting right on stage with the band."

"I know, but I didn't know how to get hold of you. You were such a big star and all. You've been gone since the end of our junior year."

"That's true. Sometimes I forget how long it's been. The sixties were such a turbulent time. One can tend to forget a lot from that era. 'If you remember the sixties, you probably weren't there,' as the old saying goes."

As we walked to the luggage carousel, we continued our reintroduction, but the tone turned a bit more serious, even if for only a moment.

"Yeah, I was going to ask you how you managed to skip out on the war. I didn't see you over there in Nam. Not that I would have, but...."

"Quite simply, they never knew where I was. I was all over the place, man. I rarely had a permanent address. We were always touring, hanging out at someone's pad, you know. I guess I just flew under the radar," he said while making a flying jet gesture with his hand. "The agency held most of my checks and forwarded me what bread I needed. I wasn't the only one, but I guess I was lucky in that respect."

"I served."

Taylor's already restrained tone turned a bit more somber. "God bless you, man. This world needs more people like you, people who are willing to stand up and be counted. I guess I was so damn selfish during those days. As I age, I see how foolish I was and how right people like you were, even with respect to that war. Sometimes, if you don't raise your fists, you'll be dropped where you stand. And seeing what's going on today, I think it applies more so."

Taylor spotted his bag and got into position to retrieve it. "There's a time and a place for everything on this planet," he said, as if making a proclamation. "It's part of the great plan, I suppose." Taylor grabbed his suitcase, despite its attempt to elude his grasp.

"So anyway...hell, let me get a look at you. I'm so busy jawing." Taylor took a quick head-to-toe once over of me. "Well, I suppose you are looking good for an old-timer. A little snow on the roof I see."

"Oh yeah, and like you were born with long, gray, thinning hair?"

"Actually, I was born with no hair, but I suppose I never was one much for change. So what's up? What's on the agenda for the day?"

"Oh, I don't know. I thought we'd head up to town and maybe grab a cold one at Walt's for old time's sake. I believe you ventured in there once or twice using your old fake draft card."

"Hah, imagine me with a draft card. But I do have to tell you, I really can't imbibe anymore. I guess I overdid things a bit back in the day, so the doc told me to lay off the hooch if I knew what was good for me."

"I see. Well, can you still go there and allow me to buy you some lunch?"

"You're on."

We traipsed through the airport, then across the parking lot to the car. As we drove, we made conversation along the way.

"So where will you be staying, Tay?"

"Oh hell, I haven't gotten that far yet. I don't know. Maybe I'll get a room at the old Blaine. I had an aunt that came to town years ago and she'd always stay there."

"No, no way, man."

"Why, what's wrong?"

"Tay, you've been gone a long time. Take it from me, not The Blaine. It's now a hangout for hos and addicts."

"Well, one out of two ain't bad," he said, adding in a laugh. "Tell you what, until I get situated, I'll just stay with you."

"Well okay. That will work for a little bit I suppose. It will give us some time to catch up."

After we hit town, I took the long way to Walt's, and swung by the old neighborhood. Perhaps it wasn't the right move, as I noticed Taylor tighten up once I turned down certain vaguely familiar streets and he realized where we were heading. To say the least, Taylor didn't have an ideal upbringing, and I realized that at the time, but I didn't know how deep that pain ran until much later.

We pulled up and stopped on Woodward, in front of the house that separated Taylor's old house and my boyhood home. I got out, and Taylor slowly followed.

"Wow, would you look at the old neighborhood? It's hard to believe that it's been nearly forty years since we roamed this area. We were the kings of the neighborhood back then, remember?"

"Yep. It seemed like all of the kids followed us. We were the ones always causing havoc around here, if I remember correctly."

"Yep, there wasn't a dare you wouldn't take. It didn't matter whether it was ringing door bells and running, toilet papering the old Pfeiffer place on a yearly basis, or egging the Zimmer's house on Halloween. Your memory is still intact."

"Unfortunately you're right, because I remember everything about this place. Right here where we're standing, I looked out my bedroom window one night and saw my mom running out to a car and get in. I figured it was another of her many boyfriends. I saw a lot of that through that window over the years. Guys claiming to be an uncle would be hanging around the house every other night while my dad was working third shift at the GM plant. My mom must have come from a very large, close home, if you catch my drift. I'll bet I had a dozen so-called uncles. It really embarrassed me because I figured all of the dudes we used to hang out with in the neighborhood knew. They just didn't say anything about it."

"Well, we all had our suspicions."

"It's funny–well, not really funny–but one day, I eventually became one of those uncles myself to God only knows how many little voyeurs. I can still see some of those kids' faces, just staring at me. A few were old enough to realize what was going on and were angry, while the rest just stood there with their teddy bear in one hand, and their free thumb in their mouth."

"I'm sorry, Tay."

"A few caught us in the act, something I was no stranger to myself. I knew exactly what they were thinking. It was like déjà vu all over again. It was like I was looking in a mirror many years removed, but I did it anyway. What comes around goes around, I suppose."

"Anyway, this one night, when I was around twelve years old, I saw Mom get in a car right here around midnight, leaving me all alone in the house. She never came back. She was gone for good. I heard Dad arguing with her on the phone from time to time, but I don't think I ever saw her again."

I knew that Taylor's mom's reputation had to have upset him back then. It was the source of his only school fight when he was in his turbulent fourth year of elementary school. Some of his fellow students had heard rumors of Mrs. Taylor's wayward ways, and his mom was branded a whore by one of the tougher kids a grade ahead of him. I believe the father of the lad in question had had relations with Mrs. Taylor at some point in time. Anyway, despite the dismal odds, Taylor did the only thing he could do in retaliation by fighting the guy just outside of Mrs. Baymont's classroom. They duked it out in the dirt area around home plate on the kickball field during lunchtime, and Taylor ended up getting pinned by the older boy. Not wanting to leave a scar and get in trouble, the tow-headed kid named Darrell verbally belittled Taylor in front of most of the class, then spit in his face. Some in the crowd that had gathered snickered at Taylor, while the rest felt sorry for him. Those scars ran deep, and– by Taylor's current tone–it was evident that the pain had yet to completely heal.

"Then of course there's the curb over here," Taylor said, as we walked towards the front of his old house. "Dad hit it almost every morning when he came home from the bar. Look at that," he said, pointing at a missing chunk of concrete. Even though the infraction

16

he spoke of had taken place many decades ago, the weathered damage remained to this day.

"I remember when he hit that portion of the curb and broke it off. He smacked it hard, almost as hard as he used to hit me. Anyway, he struck the curb so directly that he tore that chunk of concrete loose. He blew the tire off the rim as well. He got me out of bed during the early hours before I got ready for school and made me change it in the rain. I was a mess, if I recall correctly. I think we used that piece of curb for years to prop open the back door during the summer hot spells. It was a constant reminder of that unpleasant morning, that unbearable time in my life. I'll bet if we ventured on to the back porch, we'd find it sitting right there, even today."

"No, I think we've seen enough."

"Yep. Usually when you go back to your old neighborhood or school, you notice all of the things that you remember fondly. I guess not for me."

"Don't you see anything around here that brings a smile to your face?"

Taylor quickly glanced around. "No, not a thing. And for God's sake don't suggest we head back to our old elementary school. Talk about unpleasant memories. That place was the basis for my song *Early Ghosts Never Fade*."

"No, I wouldn't do that to you," I said, noting the humor of his statement. "Tell you what; let's head over to Walt's."

We got in the car and pulled away from the curb. Since we were not exactly in a comfort zone, I decided to go for broke and get all of the unpleasantries out of the way.

"Tay, are you going to visit Greenwood Cemetery while you're in town and stop by your parents' graves? You never did show up for their funerals."

"That's because I didn't find out that they were dead until just a second ago."

"Oh God, I'm sorry man, I didn't..."

Waving me off, he said, "Don't worry about it. Hell, if they were still alive, they would be damn-near ninety years old. Living as they did, I never held out hope that they would make it past seventy."

"Actually, you're pretty close."

We pulled into Walt's and exited the vehicle. Taylor arched his back, then looked around a bit. A slight smile crossed his lips.

"Man, the wild times we had here. This place looks pretty much the same. The brush has grown up a bit around the fence line, the parking lot still needs paving, and Walt still doesn't have a sign up even designating that this place is a bar, yet it always did tremendous business. If it wasn't for the Budweiser sign in the window..."

"Walt is long gone, of course, but I think they still have the same booths in here from our day, as well as the yellow stain on the ceiling from when Bobby grabbed the mustard bottle and gave it an almighty squeeze. Remember that?"

"Good Lord, doesn't anything ever change around here?"

"That, coming from a guy who hasn't altered his hairstyle in three-plus decades."

"Touché."

We entered the breezeway, then the darkened main bar, to the sounds of Frank Sinatra belting out the song *New York, New York* via the jukebox. Walt's was a throw-back to an earlier era as the same old bouquet of cherry urinal block mixed with stale beer greeted us as usual. I guess Taylor was right; some things never change. I remember that song echoing off those same walls way back when. Anyway, also awaiting us was a surprise I hadn't told Taylor about. Seated inside were three guys we used to hang with during our school years. When we walked in, they let out a whoop and a holler.

"Good God, look what the dog dragged in!" The three got up and performed the standard back slaps and head rubs, before the five of us settled in for some good old-fashioned reminiscing. We ordered up some food and had a few laughs before tackling current events.

"So Taylor, what have you been up to lately? I'll bet you're spending all of your time hanging out with all of the Hollywood stars, dating the honeys, and the like, huh?"

"Yeah, right. Perhaps many years ago, but now I just hang out and take it easy. I'm an old man now. I think all of the years of touring took their toll on me. I've about had it with music and the like. I don't even listen to the radio much anymore."

"Man, you are old. So you thought you'd come back to the old stomping grounds and…"

"And…I don't know. I'm not sure why I wanted to come back to this God-forsaken hell-hole. I ran from it back in sixty-seven. Why I'm dragging my ass back here in the two-thousands, I haven't a clue."

"I think everybody eventually returns to their roots, wherever they may be."

19

"Well, I'm here, and it's so cool to see you guys again, so that's a plus. It's like hitting a time warp, except you're all grey-haired, fat, and bald. By the way, what happened to the young crowd that used to hang in this place? Everyone in this place is so old. Look around."

"Oh, and you aren't?"

"Hell, I'm just as smooth and handsome as I was in sixty-seven."

Laughter ensued. "Tay, if you remember back then, Ohio was an eighteen state, and a good fake I D could get you in here at sixteen. Times have changed."

"Okay, so what's on the docket for the day? I don't have a clue what there is to do in this town anymore."

"Well, there really isn't anything to do around here anymore. While you were out in L.A. playing rock star, we were here working hard at becoming the rust belt capital of the U.S. About everything around here has dried up. The jobs are scarce, most of the movie theaters have closed, the factories have been torn down, and the All-American Amusement Park up the road closed up shop a few years ago."

"They closed All-American? Hell, I had some great times there. That's a damn shame. I rode The Racer roller coaster there one night with Lisa Collins, remember her, and got my first kiss from her over by the antique car ride…an hour later…while her dad was looking for her. I barely escaped with my ass. He was a mean old sucker. That was a really far out time. I wonder whatever happened to Lisa."

"I saw her at the last reunion. She's put on a little weight. Well, maybe a lot of weight. Okay, she's a bit dumpy to be honest, but aren't we all? Lisa's a grandmother now. She has been for some time. The good start young."

"Yep. The pretty ones are always the most sought after."

"I hear tell that she's now single. So Tay…"

"Don't even go there."

"I'm only saying…"

Laughter ensued.

"Thinking back, I also remember they used to have an all-summer carnival down at the east side shopping center. That was great. Don't tell me the shopping center is gone."

"No, it's still there but the carnival is no more. Hell, I think it closed down before you left town."

"I guess I didn't realize that so much can change in thirty-some years."

"Damn right, except for you. You're still bucking the trend with the long hair hippie look I see."

"Go to hell, man." Taylor then followed up that brainless remark with one of the smarter things I think I've ever heard him say. He was a man of contrasts–I'll give you that.

"I am who I am, for each man dances to his own tune." He was right.

"So that's it; there's nothing going on around here anymore?"

"Well, we could head to the VFW tonight and play some cards."

"Uh…" Taylor began.

"Taylor probably wouldn't be too welcomed in there. He didn't serve," I said.

"Didn't serve? What do you mean? Were you four-F?"

"The draft board couldn't find me," he said, with a small chuckle.

"One of those, huh? A draft dodger! You and Springsteen!"

"No, man, I wasn't a draft dodger."

"Did you hide out in England with Clinton?" Well, I'll tell you what, you're right. You wouldn't be welcomed there. In fact, I'm not real comfortable in here at the moment."

"Look man, I wasn't going to join a war that was going to mess me up like World War II did my dad."

"*Join it*? You make it sound like a giant club."

"Oh wasn't it? Wasn't it a huge killing club?"

"Hey guys!" I said, trying to cool the moment.

"Going to war screwed my dad up for life and turned him into a miserable soul. I wasn't going to let that happen to me, so you can take your all-American crap and stick it up your ass!"

"Look buddy, you can go to hell, you know that."

Steve scooted his chair back from the table, rose, then headed towards the door.

Taylor said, "Come on, man. That was like a lifetime ago."

"Steve!" I called out to him, but he kept going.

"Let him go," Taylor said. "He's still living in the past, I guess. See," he said while shaking a finger in Steve's direction, "I never wanted to end up like that, but as a result, I guess I'm not welcome in many places, even in my old hometown. Too much time has passed by, too many things have happened."

"No, that's okay, Tay. Don't worry about it. Steve's always been a little high-strung since he got back from Nam. That doesn't make him a bad person."

"He needs to grow up."

"Cut him a break, just like he should be doing for you," added Gary. "And just what is your deal? You're coming across like you're so superior to everyone around here because you're some sort of Hollywood transplant and we're just a bunch of hometown bumpkins."

"I'm sorry. Maybe you're right. I'm just a little uptight tight now. You know, jetlagged and all."

"Okay guys, let's end the debate on that. This is supposed to be a fun night. I'll tell you what, we were planning to head out to the football game tonight," I said. "My nephew is in uniform, even though he's a freshman. I told him I'd be there to watch him anyway. Friday night football hasn't changed around here. Hamilton is already off to a three-and-one start."

"Man, I haven't been to a high school game in, well, thirty-plus years. That sounds cool. I'm not particularly into the 'kids' thing, but I can still dig it. Football it is, then."

Taylor, myself, and Gary Campbell finished our dinner, left Walt's, and eventually made our way over to the football field. It's on the same grounds where we once played, me on the football team, and Taylor in the band. For him it was like a flashback, to coin a sixties term. Of course, he was a drummer, even back then, and a damn good one as I recall. I was an offensive right guard, but not a very good one. So, Taylor went on to be a career musician and I ended up pushing pencils for a living. I harkened back to what Taylor said; we all dance to our own tune.

While I saw some playing time during my senior year, Taylor had already upped and left town to seek his fortune, as they say. There were a number of variables involved in his departure. As I mentioned before, Taylor's home life was anything but a model of perfection. He was a forgotten child. Apparently, he wasn't important enough for his mother to stick around to complete the task of raising him, and he wasn't a significant enough factor in Lenny Taylor's life for him to abandon his vices and to pay proper attention to his succeeding generation.

I believe Taylor's elderly Aunt Louise was the only person in his family that held out any hope for his success. I think she said words to the effect that Taylor's view of life was a bit out of the ordinary, but it was people like that who see the other side of life and thereby attract success in larger amounts than the general populace.

In his life, Taylor's refuge was music, his music, and he threw himself into various bands from his junior high days until he left the area. He wasn't above the masses, musically speaking, to shun the school band. Taylor wanted to learn from whatever source was available. He yearned to learn and improvise, and that was the passion that drove him to become a most versatile musician.

That thirst for musical knowledge, while the driving force behind his eventual success, also became his undoing here in town. While the decision to set out on his own and leave the past behind him eventually benefited Taylor and his career, the fallout from his action negatively affected so many individuals. Taylor's parents ultimately lived out their lives in despair, not so much because they had abandoned Taylor and any prospect for a healthy family life, but

24

because his untimely exodus had deprived them of the opportunity to make amends to him before their ultimate demise.

Taylor's parents weren't the only ones affected. The straw that broke the camel's back in this situation came from a clash of creative minds. Taylor was in the high school marching band, as I said, and the band was led by a Hamilton High class of '50 grad, Bob Harmon. Bob meant well, but it was the sixties, and the standards for everything we came to know as a constant way of life was rapidly changing. What was hip and in vogue yesterday was now passé.

Clothing styles were changing from year to year as well. Politically, it was no longer acceptable to follow the status quo. The hero now wore a black hat. Change for change's sake was now the norm. To be honest, it was difficult to keep up with many of the fads and styles, and no one wanted to be left behind.

Musically, the landscape had been in constant flux since the end of World War II. The big band era was ushered out by easy listening music, then rock and roll replaced easy listening, and from then on it was said that James Brown made us shout, The Beatles made us scream, and Vulture, well, they made us absolutely wild. But, that's what the people wanted during that period.

By the time 1967 rolled around, the Fab Four were in the process of recording their *Sgt. Pepper's* album, Cream was promoting their *Disraeli Gears* LP, and The Velvet Underground was hitting its stride. Despite his youth, Bob Harmon was schooled in the traditional ways of music, typical of a university education. Taylor, however, considered himself part of the new wave of music.

It tormented Taylor to no end to see Harmon teaching his students the 'one note at a time' method, when Taylor felt that approach killed off any possibility for a song to develop a rhythm of its own. "The notes were there," he was quoted to say, "but that's only half the battle." He saw so much more potential in his fellow students, perhaps more than their instructor did.

Anyway, the two were at each other's throats constantly, and Harmon considered Taylor a distraction. Finally, near the end of our junior year, Taylor told Mr. Harmon to go to hell. Harmon kicked him out of the band, and the school suspended Tay for three days just before summer recess. When Taylor's dad found out, he literally kicked him out of the house, following a knockdown, drag out session. Since he was now on his own, Taylor saw no reason to stay around town, so he hitched a ride out to the West Coast and became a success. So goes one man's life.

It was now some three and a half decades later, and we found ourselves back at the high school where it had all begun. I guess we had come full circle, as it were.

When we entered the stadium, I noted that some things never change at a high school football game, and that's not necessarily a bad thing. The wonderful aromas of popcorn and brats, mixed with bubble gum and Teen Spirit filled the air. I always mused that if you could bottle that fragrance and distribute it to the disheartened elderly, they could open the lid when they were feeling down and out, and it would most assuredly lift their spirits as it took them back to a time when they were once young, innocent, and eager to discover all that life had to offer. End of problem.

As we wound our way through the crowd, we encountered many adults loitering about displaying lapel stickers identifying them as parents of number so-and-so on the field. It must have been Senior Night, or something along those lines. We also spotted that stout fellow who's been a mainstay at the games for years, hocking raffle tickets for some worthy cause or another, and you couldn't miss the group of little boys you always seem to see playing their pick-up football games in the end zone with the little hand-sized plastic football. I commented to Gary, "I swear those same kids must travel from game to game, city to city, and haven't aged a day from when we spotted them while we were on the field running warm-up drills."

Of course, not everything had stayed the same. I noted many differences in the stadium from our days in the sixties. The old rickety wooden bleachers had long-since been replaced by newer shiny aluminum ones, the press box had been renovated and was hardly recognizable from our day, and the dusty, dirty cinder track had become a thing of the past. The only vestige of our time was the field itself. Hamilton's field was still grass, not plastic like that which had been recently installed at a few of the more affluent schools in the area. I never liked the high crown the field sported, but it appeared as if that had finally been corrected, or perhaps it had been worn down by the passage of time and the elements.

The school itself had been enlarged as well. With over two thousand students in attendance, that number dwarfed the twelve-hundred of our day. We were probably a bit closer as a class, at least as close as four hundred-plus people can be, but there are so many additional programs available to the student population today. I would have to say that it's a six-of-one, half-dozen-of-another situation.

Hamilton was hosting South Ridgeway on this evening, and the Big Blue team, true to form, ran up a two touchdown advantage at the half. Taylor, Gary, and I were chatting amongst ourselves, catching up if you will, when the Hamilton band entered the field. That's when Taylor went off.

"What the hell's that?"

"What?" I asked. I thought he was referring to something across the way. All I saw was the band.

"Where's the rest of the band? That can't be all of them."

"No, that's it. You know band's not a big thing in this day like it was in our time. I guess there's a bit of a stigma attached to being a band geek now. That probably started back in the mid-seventies around here. Kids nowadays sit in front of the TV and play video games. They don't do band anymore."

"You have got to be kidding me. That stumbling twenty is the band? Hell, we had something like one hundred and forty members back in our day, and this place was a heck of a lot smaller. Who the hell runs that department now?"

Since I knew the history between the two men, I replied with reluctance, "Um, Bob Harmon still runs the band."

Ever since he touched back down in town, this was the most animated I had seen Taylor. "Bob Har–you've got to be kidding! That bastard has to be eighty years old. He screwed up my life, now he's gone and totaled the entire department! Harmon," he said as if his name was synonymous with Lucifer himself.

I persuaded him to hold his voice down. There was no love lost between the two men. Taylor once commented that, musically speaking, Bob Harmon never was the sharpest cob in the outhouse, whatever that means.

"Taylor, you went on and had a pretty good career, if I remember correctly," added Gary, as a bit of a verbal jab. "Perhaps you owe him a debt of gratitude."

"My ass! I got lucky. Most of these kids don't have the options afforded me. It was a different time back then. That's a damn shame. Being in a band can be one of the most rewarding experiences in a person's life–take it from me."

The band exited the field and was replaced by a larger Mustang ensemble. "Now that's a band," Taylor commented. "At least they're closer to what we were."

The game ended with Hamilton holding on to its two touchdown lead, en route to its fourth victory of the season. We walked down the stands as we prepared to make our way to the exit, and to my surprise, Taylor broke away from us, hopped the fence, and began making his way towards the field. To be honest, I didn't think he had it in him at his age, physically-speaking.

"What the hell?" was all I could say. When I saw Taylor walking rather deliberately in the general direction of Bob Harmon, I thought I had better grab Gary so we could provide a buffer between Taylor and him making an ass out of himself. Taylor was like that; he was like that as a youngster as well.

Gary and I cleared the four-foot chain link fence with a degree of difficulty. Neither one of us was as young as we once were. We did manage to catch Taylor before he made it to Harmon.

"Tay, don't do anything rash. It's not your place," Gary reminded him.

Taylor didn't even glance our way, as he continued to walk until he got within speaking distance of Bob.

Now Bob Harmon, despite his seventy-three years, was a spry and tireless man. He stood erect, almost painfully so, and usually posed with his hands behind his back. His glasses hung from a chain around his neck, but it wasn't what one would call a modern day lanyard. His beaded necklace looked like an old time glasses chain; much like his mother could have worn.

Trying to steer the situation to a friendlier level, Gary greeted Harmon with, "Hey Bob, how are you doing? It's been a while." Gary's daughter used to have class with Mr. Harmon.

"Oh, Gary Campbell, it has been a long time. How's Debbie doing?"

"Oh she's doing fine. She graduated from U C this past year…"

Taylor interrupted. "Enough of the neighborly crap. Harmon, how the hell could you let a perfectly good band go to hell and back?"

"Excuse me? Who are you?" Bob asked.

"Oh, I was sure you'd remember me. I'm the S.O.B. you kicked out of the band back in sixty-seven because you were too old-fashioned and square to open your musical heart up to the new and innovative. You didn't like having anyone around that was more musically gifted than yourself, because they exposed your own inadequacies. That was me, so you booted me from the band."

"I'm sorry, I have to ask again, who are you?"

"Damn it, I'm Taylor…er, Ross Taylor."

To be honest, I think Mr. Harmon had some inkling who he was addressing. "Well, well, if it isn't the Prodigal Son returneth."

"I'm not here looking for forgiveness, so you can can that prodigal crap, Harmon. If anyone dishonored this school, it would have to be you, and how you've squandered the talent provided to you. I would have been Ross Taylor, class of sixty-eight, but you made sure I didn't graduate just because I told you to go to hell. Well I'll do it again–for all you've done, go to hell!"

"Taylor," I said, trying to calm him and cool the situation.

"Don't shut me up. I've been waiting for thirty-some years to say that to this bastard, and I'm not going to hold back."

"Now look here…" Harmon began, then was promptly cut off.

"No, you look here. You failed back then, and you're a failure now," Taylor said with a rapid delivery. "Look at these sorry-assed kids. Hell, their uniforms are ill-fitting, you can barely hear them when they're playing, and there isn't even enough of them to fill a regular bus. They might fill a short bus, but that's reserved for you."

"Now that was uncalled for."

"Taylor, please," I pleaded.

"You showed them how to play the notes, Harmon, but you forgot to teach them how to play the music! That has to come from the spirit, that has to come from within, and that's something you neglected to grasp from the moment you started your so-called teaching career. Some things never change. Ask yourself if you've made a positive impact on any of these kids' lives. Look around. Look at them! You'll see that the answer is no. You're nothing but an irrelevant spoke in the wheel of life, as far as I'm concerned."

"Oh come on now, Taylor."

"Sorry, he needs to hear the truth."

"The truth? You wouldn't know the truth if it bit you," Harmon replied, his hands now shaking. "If I remember correctly, you were so wrapped up in your own opinions that you came to believe that they were reality, rather than the fact that your ideas were a reflection of your own warped outlook on life. I'm here to teach these kids the basics of music and the fundamentals of participating in a marching band. That's it."

"That's it? That's not good enough. If that's the best you can do, then I stand by my opinion; you're a failure."

"Oh now come on, guys," I said, making one last ditch effort to head off a permanent falling out.

"Oh, and you think you can do better?" a bug-eyed Bob Harmon asked.

"Anyone could do better! My ten-year-old kid could do better, if I had one. Anyone in his right mind could put together a marching band ten times the size of this, ten times!"

"Then God damn it, let's see you do it! I didn't take that guff of you way back when, and I won't take it from you now, you punk. I'm seventy-three and well past retirement age. I do this job because I want to, not because I have to. I don't need your crap, or any from the board. As of now, the job of bandleader is open. Any takers?"

We were all stunned and just looked at each other. Taylor, an absent figure from these parts for so long, had already created a rift within the school and a divide within the community. It was hard to believe that he had accomplished all of this in less than eight hours.

"I didn't think so," Harmon stated as he pulled off and tossed his gold whistle down at our feet having finished his oration. Now, I'm not up on band leader protocol, if there is such a thing, but Mr. Harmon's action reminded me of a wrestler's final exodus from the sport, when he takes his shoes out to the center circle and leaves them as he walks off the mat for the last time.

Bob stomped off the field, leaving us three just standing there on the sidelines of the field as the cool autumn dew began collecting on our shoulders. Passers-by who had witnessed the dispute filed past us and just stared. I was embarrassed, to say the least, but what could Gary or I do? Taylor tried his best not to stare at the ground in an attempt to kill off the awkwardness of the situation, but there were few places for him to look without feeling the shame he had brought upon himself from his ill-conceived attempt to correct a decades-old feud. He reached down and picked up the whistle, stared at it for a moment, then we turned and started towards the exit.

Chapter 2

**Take It From the Top**

*"I always seem to have a vague feeling that he is a Satan among musicians, a fallen angel in the darkness, who is perpetually seeking to fight his way back to happiness."*

~ Havelock Ellis

We said our good-byes for the evening, hopped in the car, and headed home. Taylor and I didn't talk much on the trip back to my place. We were both still a bit stunned from what had just occurred. Taylor, through his condemnation of Bob Harmon, had caused an icon within the community to 'turn in his badge,' so to speak. Bob had been educating students within the school district for nearly a half century. Everyone knew him, and nearly everyone respected him for his dedication in the classroom and his on-field performances. If Taylor planned to stick around town for a while, he would have to keep a low profile, as there would be hell to pay from those close to the situation.

"So Tay, what do you want to do tomorrow? Do you have any plans?"

"Well, if it's alright with you, I thought I'd borrow your car for half of the day to cruise around a little bit. You know, visit the old haunts, see how much things have changed, check to see it they've cleaned the bird poop off the General Hamilton statue downtown yet, those type of things."

"Uh yeah, that's okay, I suppose. Do you, uh, that is, are you able to drive, you know?"

"Despite my outward appearance, I do have a valid California driver's license. At home, I own an Aston Martin V-Twelve Vanquish. We do drive out there."

"No, I didn't mean that. I just meant that you sounded like you haven't gotten out much lately, you know?"

"I can still drive."

"Fair enough. The car is yours."

As we pulled into the driveway and got out of the car, Taylor said, "Tomorrow is Saturday isn't it?"

"That it is."

"Sorry, I'm still a little jet-lagged. I've been up since four this morning California time. I'll tell you what, how about if we cook out tomorrow night for old time's sake. I'll score the thickest T-Bone steaks I can find, and I'll even rustle up some of that great fresh corn-on-the-cob from the roadside stand over on River Road. You don't know how I've missed that. I've been dying for a taste of that for years."

"Uh, Tay, that stand hasn't been around for decades. Plus, I think all of the fresh sweet corn has long-been harvested. You might find some at the supermarket though."

"The supermarket? That crap isn't corn. That's a bunch of Florida horse feed. It's field-fresh corn or nothing. If it's out there, I'll sniff it out. I figure that as long as I can find some fresh corn at a stand, then the seasons can't change. It will always be summer, so long as there's a steak to be grilled and some sweet corn to be eaten off the cob. It's the law. Look it up," he said with a smile. "Man, I've yearned for that delicacy forever, and as close as I am now, I'm not about to give up. If you look hard enough for what you want in life, you'll find it."

Taylor was right about one thing; the next day was ideal for a fall cookout. The sky displayed that beautiful, clear October blue, temperatures were to peak out in the mid-seventies during the day, and the forecast called for near-seventy degree dinner-time temperatures. Since the death of my wife last December, I hadn't done much in the way of entertaining. I really hadn't done much of anything to be frank. I missed that.

I rooted around the shed and pulled out the old grill. I dusted it off, found an unopened bag of charcoal briquettes, and something that could double as lighter fluid. I spent the day cleaning the house as this was the first time I would be entertaining since Janice's passing.

Taylor drove off around mid-morning into a town he hadn't visited since his young adulthood over three decades ago. Hamilton is a very typical Midwest industrial town. Much of its manufacturing base has eroded away with the times, regulations, and economic factors. As a result, its downtown now is a haven for city and county operations, as well as banks and attorneys' offices. The few remaining limestone ten-stories-and-under 'skyscrapers,' presently absent of most of the storefronts and small shops they once proudly displayed, still showed evidence of Hamilton's one-time economic prominence.

I worried about Taylor, not just because of his unfamiliarity with the area, but to be honest, I didn't know how much all of his drug use during his playing days had affected his long-term cognitive skills. He was so thin. Yes, I worried about him. Still, a skyrocketing insurance rate I didn't need, especially at my age, but I trusted him nonetheless.

I had no idea where he was going, and I'm not sure he did at first, but I eventually found out. Despite what he said earlier, Taylor did indeed stop by Greenwood Cemetery. He inquired at the front desk as to the whereabouts of his parents' graves, found out they had been interred in section 'X,' then got back into the car to drive to the site.

Taylor parked along the curb, got out, then tried to get his bearings as he turned the map this way and that in his attempt to figure out which direction north was. He found a solution by comparing the shape of the section on the map to the one at his feet. Once he figured out where he was, he cut across the grounds for about fifty yards, nearly stumbled over a walnut casing until he kicked it out of his way, then finally came to a large elm tree. He brought no flowers and no Styrofoam crosses as an offering of love and remembrance. Taylor wasn't in a compassionate mood. He glanced down, and sure enough, there was a stone marking each of the final resting places of Leonard Taylor and Ellen Paulson.

Despite a different last name for his mother, Taylor guessed that since the burial space had been purchased by the two before their split-up and her apparent remarriage, seeing that the two were never rich, they probably went ahead and used the plots anyway. What did it matter at this point? Their graves were marked by identical yet simple twelve by twenty-four inch leaf-stained gray granite ground markers with only enough information to satisfy a casual passer-by. Taylor saw that his father passed three years before his ex-wife, but nothing else. He had no idea who made the eventual burial arrangements, but his mother still had family in the area, as far as he knew. As for Lenny, well, Taylor wasn't sure about that one.

He stared at the dry and somewhat barren plots for quite a spell and noted that it must have been a rough summer weather-wise. The heat had taken its toll on nearly everyone and everything as any living vegetation had long since vacated the surrounding sod. A desert-like crack in the earth carved its way across the ground until Lenny Taylor's headstone halted its progress. Taylor stood there and ran through his head what he could say, should say, or even feel after all of these years.

"Well, you finally took time out to rest after a lifetime of running around, carousing, and other selfish behavior," he began. Taylor was a little taken aback when it dawned on him that what he was describing was exactly the type of person he himself had become. He spoke a little louder in order to silence the castigating voices within his soul. "It would have been nice to have gotten to know you a bit better than the twelve years I had with you," he said, looking towards his mother's stone, "and the seventeen years I spent with you," he said, now glancing towards his father's place, "but I'm guessing that I did get to know the real Taylors. Not a pretty picture, huh?" The more Taylor spoke, the more it became apparent that their path in life mirrored his own to a degree. Taylor continued to try to silence the voices emanating from within.

"I'm guessing you two had better things to do in life than to care for and about me. Too bad you're not around today to give me some psycho-babble about how you were hurt in your childhood and therefore 'acted out,'" he said, crooking his fingers like quote marks, "in your adulthood. I know about your childhoods. Neither one of you admitted to any abuse, so you don't have that as an excuse."

"Just because you grew up in a home with a repressive father gave you no right to play catch-up at our expense," he said, looking towards the stone bearing the name of his mother. "You soiled our

38

family name, and embarrassed me countless times through your whorish behavior."

Looking towards his father's marker, he continued, "Your time in the war might have messed you up, Pop, but at some point in time, you had to suck it up and get on with life. You never did. You didn't even try. You used it as a crutch. You wanted the world to cater to you and your needs. Maybe that's why Mom began looking around for greener pastures, you know."

Taylor, at this moment, became a little embarrassed and quite agitated, and glanced around as all his feelings seemed to come to a boil. Perhaps he was looking to see if there was anyone nearby to hear his rants.

"If you all had problems, why the hell did you even have a kid?" he said as his voice rose another decibel. He unwittingly twisted his map up as he continued. "It's bad enough that you screwed up your own lives, but you didn't have to have me and mess me up for eternity! That's what you did, you know? You imparted upon me a shell of a soul, then added, 'You're on your own, Buster. Have fun.' You could have helped guide me through this terrible thing called life, but instead you gave up on me to take care of yourselves and your own little piddly problems. I'll never know what I could have become because of that. I had to figure everything out on my own. I'll never forgive you for that. I would rather that you just didn't bother some fifty-plus years ago, but I guess I'm stuck here, aren't I? A hell of a deal, believe me. I hope you're right where you belong and the heat is turned up." After a pause, Taylor concluded in a softer, more sober voice, "I guess I'll find out soon enough, huh?"

He stood there for another moment, trying to come up with additional barbs to throw his parents' way, but decided it would be a waste of time. The deed was done and he had spent his rage. He tossed the wadded-up map into a wire flower disposal can chained to the elm, then got in the car and left.

Taylor drove around town, just to burn up time while attempting to clear his head. He cruised past the site of his old junior high school, but it was no longer there. It was now a retirement home. He drove past the old junior high school football field. That's where he had cut his teeth when it came to it came to marching bands. It had been bulldozed as well. There was an industrial park going in there now. Taylor realized that *he* was one of the few things from his past that was left standing.

While he hoped this drive would help heal his soul, seeing so much of his former life disappear took Taylor from feeling bummed out, as they used to say, to feeling downright depressed. So, instead of looking for ways to cheer himself up, he indulged in his pity party a bit longer by dropping by his old elementary school, something he also said he would refuse to do.

He pulled into the circle, got out and looked the school grounds over. Ghosts of schoolyard bullies and verbal torment from days gone by came flooding back to him, but he blew them away with a blink of an eye. Despite the tough times that he experienced on those grounds, he concluded that his treatment at the hands his fellow students had probably not been atypical.

Taylor walked around the empty school building, and stopped to glance through the entry doors of one of the three hallways. He continued on, turned the corner, and stopped to peer through the windows of his fourth grade classroom. He remembered all too well the cruelty he had suffered at the hands of his aforementioned former teacher, Mrs. Baymont. Whether they want to admit it or not, teachers do have their pets and their rivals. The rest of us fit somewhere in the middle. For whatever reason, Mrs. Baymont had Taylor in her sights.

At that time, Mrs. Baymont was under a lot of pressure, dealing with a number of disruptive students that had been recently bussed in from a low income district. Even back then, it was considered politically incorrect for a teacher to pick on a minority student, even if the situation warranted disciplinary action. Being nothing more than an average kid back then–the most average, in fact–Taylor became an easy target, so she used him as an out, the same way many of his fellow students did.

During that year, Taylor learned that his music teacher, Miss Francis, wanted to recommend him to the city's Honor Chorus, but when asked, Mrs. Baymont refused to endorse the choice saying that Taylor's singing and academic abilities wouldn't fit in with the city's best and brightest. She determined that Taylor was too bright for the remedial classes, and not motivated enough for the typical mainstream, but they placed him there anyway due to the lack of a third option. As far as his singing ability went, Mrs. Baymont commented to Miss Francis that Taylor's singing, in her opinion, was akin to, as she put it, an old sow rubbing her butt up against a splinter. She might have been raised on a farm in Kentucky, and even though she often brought that fact up to lighten the moment, that certainly gave her no excuse for the rudeness she so often displayed.

It was then and there that Taylor decided to abandon singing and take up the drums. Around that time, I remember, he took over Joe Reinhart's paperboy route on the weekends giving Joe a welcomed relief. He was happy to pay Taylor and take the time off as the Sunday *Cincinnati Enquirer* arrived at four AM, and as is typical of Sunday newspapers, it was always a killer to haul around. That was a time when paperboys piled the newspapers into a huge satchel, and either walked or biked them around the neighborhood. He could bike the Saturday edition, but had no choice other than to walk the Sunday papers around and heave it on to the doorstep. That was an especially difficult task in the winter months.

Taylor used the money to pay for drum lessons down at Imhoff's Music Store every Tuesday afternoon after school. So in the end, I guess it was Taylor who had the last word on both of the former subjects.

Having silenced the echoes from the past, Taylor got back in the car and began his search for the farm fresh corn he had promised. He drove past the site of the old River Road produce stand and discovered that I was right. Even after all of these years, the gravel pull-off was still visible through the weeds, but the shack had long since capitulated to the elements. The area had become quite overgrown and had nearly returned to its natural state.

Taylor then remembered that he had a couple of school friends who used to pick corn during the summer recess out on some of the Venice farms south of there, so he headed in that direction. Sure enough, shortly after clearing the lone stoplight in town, Taylor found a produce stand that carried a mish-mash of fresh end-of-the-season farm goods, along with traditional fall favorites such as apples, cider, and pumpkins of every size and shape. There must have been an acre of those gourds lying about providing a seasonal carroty frame for the stand.

As I recall, I had visited that market once or twice as a boy. While the produce was fantastic during the growing season, it was an absolute treat to stop there during the fall. If memory serves, there were bushel baskets lining the walls of the stand filled with every type of apples imaginable. The fragrances from the Red, Golden Delicious, and Granny Smith apples combined to create a heavenly scent that I still fondly harken back to. It was almost as if I was able to breath in local orchard owner Ainsley Singleton's apple cider; an excellent beverage he made using his own secret combination of those three apple varieties. Now at that time, I had only a vague notion what the term ambrosia meant. I came across that word when reading a story about Greek mythology once. After my first taste of this autumn cocktail, I was convinced that Mr. Singleton's cider had to come pretty close to fulfilling that definition.

Anyway, Taylor pulled into the gravel parking lot and waited for the dust to settle a bit. It didn't take long as it was a dry, slightly breezy fall afternoon. Taylor exited the vehicle and arched his back. He looked around at the landscape he had nearly forgotten. It hadn't changed much. Nothing changes much in Venice. Some of the houses had been there since the turn of the century, the last century that is, and the farms are as they were. About a quarter of a mile in the distance, Taylor spotted a John Deere tractor turning under the remnants of the past growing season. A russet cloud followed.

Taylor approached the counter, dodging a couple of children and a mutt as he went, and inquired about the availability of his favorite veggie. It was on hand, the lady at the register told him, but this was the last of the niblets for the year. He paid for a dozen ears, picked up six steaks at the nearby market, and returned back to my place. I was pleased to see that he made it back home unscathed, and the car unscratched.

It was a fantastic night, as I had invited a few friends over for the cookout. Taylor was right; it's never too late in the season to hold a barbecue. In fact, preparing the evening's feast during this time of year produced a wonderfully mixed airborne bouquet of grilled steaks and drying maple and sycamore leaves. That night, I came to agree with Taylor that charcoaled steaks are always a treat, no matter what time of the year it is. On top of that, the corn was surprisingly good, perhaps the best I've ever had. There's something to be said for maturity.

"Sometimes nature saves its best for last," Taylor said. It was good to see that he hadn't forgotten his roots.

This evening wasn't just a welcome home get-together for Taylor. It was good for me to get back into the swing of things as well. As the night grew old, we bid the others farewell, then finally had some down time between ourselves.

"I'll tell you what," Taylor began, "let me use the car tomorrow to shop for an apartment or condo, then I'll see about getting myself some transportation of my own. I don't want to be a burden to you. I probably already have."

I was taken back a bit by his suggestion. "Tay, you're no burden. You're only going to be here a few more days, aren't you?" Taylor stared at me, and his statement took root. "Are you telling me that you're actually considering settling down here?"

"For a little bit. Apparently, I have obligations now. I didn't think Harmon would freak out and bolt from the band, so now I guess I have to make good on the situation."

"I see. How about if you hold off on that. On Monday, we really need to drop in and see the principal and find out where we go from here. If they don't allow you in, the entire thing might be a moot point. Maybe Harmon is just blowing smoke."

Harmon wasn't blowing smoke. He was done. We called the school's principal, Charles Dooley, around nine AM that Monday, but Harmon had already beat us to the punch. Mr. Dooley agreed to meet with us, but judging from the tone of his voice, I didn't think that cordiality was tops on his list at this point. Taylor was in no position to dictate the terms of the get-together, so we were at the mercy of Mr. Dooley's schedule. He ordered an eleven o'clock meeting.

Taylor was nervous about entering the school he had abandoned so long ago, having to fend off all the negativity that still roamed the halls and all, so he was none too pleased about subjecting himself to this déjà vu experience. Some memories never die, as they say, and they're usually referring to the painful memories. Taylor was also uneasy about the one-on-one with Mr. Dooley, especially considering the circumstances for the get-together, so he doted on his physical presentation.

"How do I look? Acceptable?"

"Acceptable, but if you want my honest opinion, it would help your case if you got a haircut or something."

"No time, plus I haven't worn my hair short since my dad used to give me a burr way back when. He used, I think, some old dog clippers, so I don't intend to become something I'm not. I am who I am."

"Suit yourself."

We arrived at the school and made our way through the hallways, past curious onlookers who could only speculate who these old geezers were and what they were doing in their school. Like I said, some things never change.

The clapping of the shoes on those old multi-flecked marble floors from the masses as they rushed between classes in an attempt to beat the bell were the same as I always remembered. I'm sure that was true for Taylor as well.

We were directed to the office and were told to take a seat on one of those hard, varnished hickory chairs that have probably been around as long as the school has. These were the same chairs a student had to sit in before being escorted into the vice-principal's office for swats, in our day, or to be awarded a detention, at the present time. I believe, to this day, that those old hickory chairs are virtually indestructible.

Finally, Principal Charles Dooley came around the corner, and with a barely audible grunt, motioned us with a quick flip of his wrist towards his office. Charles Dooley was a balding, soon-to-be barrel-chested man in his late forties. He sported a mustache that befitted him, and was dressed in a starched white shirt. That suited him as well.

Principal Dooley emerged from a high school era other than Taylor and me. He graduated in the mid 1970's-a post-Vietnam War graduate. His reputation was one of 'firm but fair.'

We entered the smallish office and looked for a seat. The frosted window rattled in its frame as he shut the heavy wooden door behind us. I had met Mr. Dooley once before and mentioned the fact to him as we all took our seats. Dooley barely acknowledged the meeting and treated the journey down memory lane as a sour afterthought.

"Which one of you is Taylor?" he asked after clearing his throat.

"That would be me," Taylor answered while raising his hand slightly. After all, this *was* school. Mr. Dooley glanced up to see who he was addressing, then did a double take as if it was the first time he laid eyes on Taylor. It might have been.

"Uh huh," he said as he shuffled a few papers. He then looked up and addressed Taylor directly. "Do you mind telling me where you get off chewing out one of this school's icons," and then with a louder voice he continued, "causing him to resign in the middle of the season? Who the hell are you anyway?"

"Mr. Dooley," I began, but was shortly cut off.

"I'm not talking to you. I'll get to your explanation for being here later. I'm talking to the old hippie here."

"Hey, now there's no need for name calling," I said.

"Oh, and why not? It seems your friend here has no problem tossing out the verbal barbs at seventy-year-old men when it suits him. What's good for the goose is good for the…what, who are you? Explain yourself."

"Sir, I'm Taylor Ross, and the argument I got into with Mr. Harmon probably should have taken place some thirty years ago when I was one of his students. Some things never die, you know?"

"No, I don't know. All I do know is that I'm now out a band instructor. There's no way we can move people around at this stage of the game and make a decent showing for the second half of the season. You've ruined everything!"

"From what I could tell, they weren't making much of a showing as it was. That was the basis for our argument. How many people are in the band anyway? Twenty?"

"Twenty-eight to be exact, at least there were. Two of them came here this morning and said that they planned to drop out. Without a leader, many, if not most of them, might drop out, and what will that do to their scholarship chances? Many of them receive scholastic credit for band, and if they're close when it comes to graduation, that lost credit might cost them their diploma. Did you ever give any thought to that?"

"I'm sorry sir, but…"

"But nothing. You come to settle an ages-old argument with a former teacher, and in the process, screw up a lot of people's lives. What have you got to say for yourself?"

"Sir, I see the dilemma you're left with here. If it's any consolation, I can teach these kids band."

"You? You've got to be kidding! What the hell do you know about music?"

"I was with a rock band for seventeen years. You might have heard of them, Vulture?"

"Vulture?"

"Yes. We sold over seventy-five million albums worldwide, Mr. Dooley, so I think I know a little something about music."

"Vulture? Which one were you again?

"I was the percussionist, the drummer."

"Oh wait now, you're the one who used to do a flip off the drum stand at the end of the concert, am I right?"

"On occasion. The only problem was, the older I got, the higher they had to raise the stand because, well, I got older."

"Yeah, and you missed a few of those flips as I recall."

"In my less-than-lucid moments."

"Well that explains a lot. Hell, I didn't recognize you. Holy moley, you are him. I'll be damned. It's an honor to meet you," he said while raising up from his chair and reaching across his desk to shake Taylor's hand. "So what have you been doing with yourself for the past decade or so?"

Being a little nervous, Taylor answered, "Um, well you know, I've mostly been advising cohorts in the business, sitting in with production crews and the like."

"Fantastic." I was relieved to see that Mr. Dooley's mood had changed towards us. He did return to a serious, but less than angry, disposition when asking, "Be that as it may, we're still left with a significant hole to fill when it comes to the band. You know what an icon Bob Harmon is in this community."

"Mr. Dooley..."

"Call me Chuck."

"Um, Chuck, since I got us into this mess, I'll do what I can to help out with the band. I can lead the band if that's what you need, and make it bigger and better than it has been in decades. I guarantee it."

"Well, that's very generous Taylor, but there are legalities involved here. I just can't throw you out there and say, "Have at it." Have you ever been certified as a music instructor?"

"Well no, but I know out west they allow qualified personnel," he said making quote marks with his index and middle fingers, "to take on non-full time positions like coaches and such. Hopefully, that applies here as well. I come cheap."

"That's all well and good, but I'll have to check with the board on this. I have to say that I have my doubts, though. There are legalities, as I said, and state regulations to fulfill, and I don't even want to get into the insurance aspect of this."

"My guess is that we have to do something fast. There's a road game over in Middletown coming up this Friday."

"I'm well-aware of that, but I do have to ask you one thing: Do you think you can actually pull it off? I mean, do you know anything about leading a marching band? You're used to a five-piece ensemble, not dozens of kids performing music and marching in formations."

"I realize that, but we're still left with a problem: If I don't do it, who will? Yes, I'll need them to teach me as much as I'll lead them, but hopefully, I can bring some spirit to an institution that has been dying for decades."

"Okay, I'll look into it and get back with you within the day. Here," he said while shoving a legal pad over in Taylor's direction. "Give me your name, address, and phone where you can be reached. Time is of the essence."

As he wrote, Taylor tossed out an idea. "I hope those two students don't leave the band. Talk to them, Mr. Dooley, and tell them fresh new help is on the way. They won't be sorry. Also, I had an idea. Is there any way the school can hold an assembly of some kind in the next day or so and try to sell the kids on the virtues of being in the band?"

"I suppose so, but how will you convince two thousand students that it's cool to be in a band? In my opinion, you're trying to turn water into wine."

"That's what I planned on. I have some ideas. Here, here's my number," he said as he shoved the pad in Mr. Dooley's direction, "and I want you to call me today regardless and we'll set something up for Wednesday or Thursday with respect to an assembly."

"Will do. Thanks, Taylor."

We walked out of the front office and back into the crowded
hallways. We both leaned up against the ceramic-coated cinder block
wall and breathed a sigh of relief. We watched as students ran to and
fro and slammed their lockers. We nearly jumped out of our skins as
the bell right above our heads sounded alerting everyone that second
lunch about to begin. Be that as it may, we managed to escape with
our nerves and our butts intact.

As we walked to the car, I asked Taylor, "So what's your great
plan for the assembly?" Taylor didn't respond. He acted as if he
didn't hear me and just looked away. "You don't have one, do you?"

He looked straight ahead and said quietly, "Oh Lord, I've really
opened a flock of worms with this one, haven't I?" He turned to me.
"Hell, I don't even like kids. I really can't stand being around the
little buggers, to be honest with you. I hated being a kid, and I barely
tolerated the teeny-boppers who used to follow the group. I just
never was on their level, you know what I mean? I guess I was never
allowed to be young. You're right on, Smitty. I'm in way over my
head here."

"Okay, but there's no need to panic. If the board lets you in–and
that's a big if, let's face it–then all you have to do is hold the status
quo for another six weeks. After that, the band pretty much shuts
down for the year and you'll be off the hook. They might do an
occasional post-season competition, but with just over two dozen
members, it's not likely that they really have a legitimate chance at
any winning any of those."

We left and headed for home. Taylor spent much of his time on
the computer pecking around the internet trying to bone up on
marching band formations and techniques. It was his 'crash course,'
if you will. Around two-thirty that afternoon, Mr. Dooley called and

wanted to see us immediately; well, actually he wanted to see Taylor. I told him to go and let me know what happened. "I guess I'm not your manager anymore." I flipped him the keys. "Take the car."

Just as the students were filing on to their respective buses at the end of the school day, Taylor shimmied his way past the crowd on his way to the office. Mr. Dooley passed him and told him he'd be with him shortly, so Taylor entered Dooley's office and took his now-familiar seat. Taylor sat there for five minutes, spending his time squinting at the diplomas on the opposite wall and trying to gooseneck a peek at the papers on the principal's desk. Despite the fact that Mr. Dooley's office used to be the guidance counselor's old office, it still reminded Taylor of the old days. He spent some time in the principal's office, but almost no time in the guidance counselor's office.

Finally, Mr. Dooley returned, with a woman in tow. "Taylor, I'd like you to meet Kaylee Lewis." Taylor rose and offered his hand. "Kaylee is a health instructor here at Hamilton and has run the flag corps for the last four years. She's here to help us all out."

Kaylee was a neat lady. An attractive woman in her own right, she was around thirty years of age, and still possessed a fairly athletic form on her five foot six inch frame. Her longer than shoulder length ginger hair gave her an engaging look. Highlighting her facial features was an appealing, round cherry mouth which could easily ripen into a cheerful smile under the right conditions. Despite having left her teen years a decade or so ago, her fair skin still sported a small cluster of freckles on either side of her nose.

The three sat down and Mr. Dooley explained the current situation. "Taylor, I took your case directly to Donald Morgan up at the board and discussed what we wanted to do. He explained simply that it wasn't possible for you to take over the band without a State of Ohio certification. Those are the rules, but there is also a legal liability on our part. If we were a private school, or even one of the poorer districts, the board might turn a blind eye, but that isn't the case here."

"That's a bummer. So we're screwed then?"

"Not necessarily. That's why I asked Ms. Lewis to help us out. You see, Ms. Lewis is a state certified employee of this district, and since she has considerable knowledge of the band and its operation, we can appoint her to the head position, and take you on as, say, a volunteer. That is, if you're willing to perform this job gratis."

"Yeah, money's no problem. It sounds like there might be some problem with stepping on some toes though," he said with a touch of cynicism in his voice. Taylor was his own man, and his personal history didn't include playing back-up to 'some chick,' as he put it. Much of his respect for adult women in a position of authority had dissolved after his mother parted ways with the Taylor family.

"That shouldn't be a problem. I'm only there for legal purposes. You're the one with all of the musical knowledge," she shot back with an equal touch of sarcasm, knowing full well that Taylor's background was limited to a five-piece combo.

Either he was oblivious to the tension between the two individuals across from him, or perhaps he was eager to wrap the situation up. Either way, Mr. Dooley was satisfied with the new beginning and brought the meeting to a close.

As the two exited the office, Ms. Lewis told Taylor, "Come on down to my office and I'll fill you in on my ideas for running the band until we get a permanent replacement."

Taylor was uncomfortable with the situation already. "If I'm supposed to run the band and you're just supposed to be a figurehead, will you be interested in any of my ideas?"

"In time. Until then, we have to keep things up and running as we have a game coming up Friday night."

"In time? Look missy…"

"Look man, dude, or whatever you want to be called…"

"Hey, mellow out, babe. Taylor, call me Taylor. All I ask for is a little respect."

"Fine, Taylor, but ditto that. Respect begets respect. You got that? I'm sure you're ready to call me all sorts of things right now, but for the time being, you can call me Kaylee. To be brutally honest, right now I'd prefer Ms. Lewis from you."

"Oh, a hothead. I like that in a babe."

"Judging from your attitude, I doubt you truly like women. Let me guess, you like women if they…cater to your needs…bow down to you…throw their panties on the stage while you rock out?"

"Hey, I don't need this."

"Oh yes you do," she said as she stopped in the hallway and faced Taylor directly. "You deserve all of this. You chased off one of the all-time favorite teachers from this school. You'll be lucky if anyone even speaks to you during your stint here. And if all you learn from this experience is that women can be your equal, well then Buster you've learned one of life's great lessons."

"Oh, so that's how it's going to be, huh? You're going to fight me the whole way on this thing? I see. You're doing me a favor? Favors I don't need."

"No, but you do need me. Without me, you aren't even allowed to set foot on campus. So it's in your best interest to fall into line and know where your place is."

"Damn, can you be anymore patronizing?"

"If you continue to be part of the problem rather than the solution, just watch me."

The two stomped down the hallway and into the health office, which was right next to the locker rooms. Kaylee threw her folders down and took a seat behind the desk.

Taylor just stood in the doorway. "Where's my desk?" he asked.

"Your desk? You're only going to be here for the next five or six weeks, and the majority of time you'll be out in the field."

"What if I need to keep some paperwork here or something like that?"

In a fit of frustration, Kaylee tore her multi-stack in-and-out trays apart, ripped the label off one of them, and slammed it down in the corner by Taylor's hand.

"There, that's your tray, and you can use the chair next to you. That corner is your desk. Congratulations on your promotion."

"Oh nice, I get the kiddies' table. Look, clear something up for me; why the resentful attitude towards me? What the hell did I ever do to you?"

Kaylee slammed her pen down and lit into Taylor. "You come into this town, make a favorite teacher resign, then I end up getting this job dumped in my lap. I barely have enough time to do my own job, and now I have to spend my Friday nights out on some high school field trying to hold together what's left of a band that you nearly destroyed! So look buddy-boy, you're going to do the major share of the work around here because, plain and simple, I don't have the time."

"I would think you'd have all of the time in the world."

"Come again?"

"Well, I mean, a pretty girl like you, twenty-thirty-something, and you have your Friday nights available to occupy yourself with a band. Sounds like there's an emptiness you're trying to fill there." Taylor's face brightened. "Ah, now it all fits. Now I know where the hostility is coming from. You're not getting any." Taylor chuckled. Kaylee wasn't amused, to say the least.

"Get out!"

"Get out? I must have struck a nerve, huh? The truth hurts sometimes."

With gritted teeth, she demanded, "Get out of this office, you narrow-minded jackass! The less we see of each other, the better!"

"Where am I supposed to go?"

"Go to hell, for all I care!" After a pause and neither one flinched, Kaylee let loose again. "You've got a band waiting on you. Go down to the band room and get them organized and out on the field!"

"Yes ma'am." Taylor stood and presented her with a mock salute. He exited the room, but just after ten seconds, he stuck his head back in the door.

"Um, hey big Lew, just where is the band room?"

She picked up her desk calendar and threw it Taylor's way with his head being the intended target. Taylor slammed the door but could hear her muted voice yell, "Find it yourself. You seem to know everything!"

Chapter 3

## A Symphony of Errors

*"A woman's two cents worth,*

*is worth two cents in the music business. "*

~ Loretta Lynn

Taylor walked the hallways towards what used to be the industrial arts wing of the school and encountered a teacher heading in the opposite direction. She seemed to be a bit startled at seeing an adult of Taylor's stature, dressed as he was in his old ratty denim jacket and jeans to match. He appeared more like a homeless man rather than an interim bandleader wandering the hallways of an otherwise secure school building. Despite Taylor's explanation that Ms. Lewis had sent him in search of the band room, the instructor was still a bit skeptical. Still, she pointed Taylor in the general direction, but didn't completely take her eyes off of him until he opened the door and entered.

When Taylor entered, the mood echoed that of a morgue rather than the usual uplifted manner that typically resonated from within those four walls. Students were sitting around on the risers, some spitting forth a few noted from their horns, while the rest just sat and talked. They were uncertain of what lay ahead for the band and their musical futures.

"Hey guys, what's happening? I'm Taylor Ross from the band Vulture."

Everyone looked up, but no one said anything. Vulture hadn't been a musical force to be reckoned with since before most of these kids had been born. Taylor belonged to their parents' generation, at least.

Finally, a clarinet player spoke up. "You're the one who got Mr. Harmon fired, aren't you?"

"Mr. Harmon wasn't fired. He resigned."

"Yeah, but you made him. I heard that argument you two had after Friday night's game. You called us a bunch of nobodies."

"I only meant that I thought that, uh, you were a good bunch, but Mr. Harmon hadn't tapped your full potential. I'm thinking I can do that."

"Oh yeah, and what makes you think you can do that? How many bands have you led?"

"Just one, for the most part. John Winston formed our band Vulture, and he was the leader for the first few years, but then he became more interested in wine, women, and, well, not song, but you get my drift. I pretty much took over from there and led us to our most successful years."

"How many CDs did you sell?"

"Well, they were albums in those days, but let's just say that we sold over seventy-five million units, and they're still selling. That's as many as Aerosmith."

"Who's Aerosmith?"

"Uh, yeah. Think Britney. That's pretty close, although it was a smaller world music-wise back in my day. Tell you what, let's see what you guys are working on for this week's show, and we'll take it from there."

"It's the same old stuff we do every week. We have four numbers, and we generally do three of them during any given week. The fourth number we throw in every other week to mix things up a bit."

"I see. Well, then what did you need Mr. Harmon for?"

"What do we need you for?"

Taylor saw that he had his work cut out for him. He had the band run through their numbers and pronounced them fit for the week's presentation. Their show rarely deviated from week to week, except when they had two consecutive home games. Even the parents said that if you've seen their production once, you've seen it enough.

Taylor thought that his best approach would be to try and make friends with the little scoundrels. A group of friends can take him a lot farther than any one enemy.

"Okay, if I were to ask you what we should do to recruit more members, what would you say?"

"You don't have a clue how to run a band, do you?"

"Look you little b…okay look, let's try this again. We don't want to get off on the wrong foot here. Let me ask you, why are you in the band?"

"Credit," came one response, followed by the same answer from another.

"Okay, fair enough. At least you were honest. Let me rephrase the question. If you weren't in the band, what would make you want to join?" Taylor drew stares. "Anybody? You don't have to all speak up at once." He didn't draw any laughs either. He let out a sigh, then began pulling anything and everything out of mid-air.

"Tell you what, are any of you here in any kind of band other than this; a rock band perhaps?" One of the drummers raised his hand. "Good, good. Now we're getting some place. Um, are they any good?"

"Yeah, we play gigs once or twice a month. We can bring it if we have to."

"Great. Could you bring the guys and meet here tomorrow after school?"

"I'd have to ask, but if it's worth it, they might agree. Why do you want us here?"

"Get a load of this; an assembly. Not just an ordinary pep assembly, mind you, but also a recruitment assembly, a rock assembly; huh, how about that, a rock assembly! We'll have your rock band firing the crowd up, we tell them how cool it is to be in the band, how they get to go to the game for free, hanging out together, doing road trips and all. We'll have this room so full of people afterwards that we'll have to knock out a wall just to hold them all."

The young man thought for a moment. "Maybe."

"Just think of all of the free publicity you guys will get."

"Maybe."

"Just be here tomorrow and we'll see if you all can carry a tune." Taylor leaned down to the drummer and said in a low voice, "On top of that, there's fifty bucks in it for each of you."

Taylor arrived home around six and told me of the poor start he had made with Ms. Lewis. He was distraught. I tried to be the peacekeeper as much as possible, and relayed the old adage of keeping his friends close, and his enemies closer, but Taylor had his own way of doing things.

The following day, Taylor cleared the assembly with Mr. Dooley. Dooley actually liked the idea, as it had been some time since they had had a real pep rally. Taylor was going out on a limb with this one in more ways than one, though. First, he cleared the assembly before he had even heard the rock band. He assumed that if they weren't any good, he could always use the marching band, and they could play the school song umpteen times to fire up the crowd. Plus, he didn't bother to float the idea past Ms. Lewis first.

The band showed up, did a few rehearsal numbers, and Taylor found them to be pretty decent. Actually, he said later, he was quite impressed with them. Their equipment was so much more sophisticated than what he and his fellow Vultures had started out with. With the advanced keyboards of today, it made sounding good almost easy. He just hoped that at this point, he could make an impact on the student body with the marching band as much as the rock band made an impression on him.

Just after lunch the next day, Taylor was helping to convert the gymnasium into a stage for the assembly. That's when Kaylee arrived on the scene and confronted a student who was assisting in the set-up.

"What's all of this?"

"The pep assembly, Ms. Lewis. Didn't they tell you?"

"No, I haven't had time to read my emails yet today." In a stern voice, she asked, "And who approved this?"

Taylor walked over and answered, "Principal Dooley. He thought it was a great idea."

"Oh he did, did he? And just who brought up the suggestion?"

"Yours truly." Taylor said this with a bit of cockiness, as he could tell from Kaylee's voice that she wasn't pleased at all about being kept out of the loop on this.

"Oh really, and just who gave you the authority to demand something, anything?"

With a smug attitude and his thumbs in his armpits as if gripping a set of suspenders, he replied, "I don't need any authority. I'm the band director."

Kaylee's blood was boiling about now. "Listen here you, you have no authority to do anything around here without clearing it with me first. Do you hear me?"

A student butted in. "Aw come on, Ms. Lewis. It's going to be fun."

"You stay out of this or I'll issue you a detention!" Turning back to Taylor, she continued, "I'll ask you again, have you got it? Me first."

"Me, first? Is that all you ever think about, your ego? You're so blinded by your own sense of self-worth that you're not even considering the students here. You're in a me, me, me mode. Try to think about someone or something other than yourself for once."

Positioning herself just inches from his face, she continued, "Don't you dare question my authority around here. It was your fault that we're in this position in the first place. Two wrongs don't make a right."

"What I'm doing is right. What you're doing is meddling."

"Well, I'll just have to see Principal Dooley and see about getting you removed from this position. You're obviously not fit to lead. Either you go, or I will."

"Nanner, nanner, nanner," Taylor said as an immature comeback. The students did their best to stifle a laugh. Just after Kaylee stomped off, Taylor let loose with a, "Me-me-me-me!" in a faux operatic voice. He was going over big with the students, and that was part of his plan.

Kaylee did go to Principal Dooley's office and voiced her complaint. Her ultimatum didn't quite sell itself. You see, Dooley knew she couldn't direct the band by herself. She didn't have the time or the know-how. On top of that, there was no one else around to help her out. Taylor, on the other hand, had no clue about the scholastic operations of a band, and he just plain wasn't qualified to go it alone. Principal Dooley, being the fair man that he was, told Kaylee that he would take care of Taylor and asked for her patience and understanding.

Taylor did get an ear full from the principal and agreed to 'play fairly' for the remainder of his time there, seeing how it was just a month and a half until the season commenced.

The powers that be went ahead with the assembly, and true to Taylor's word, it was a spectacle that the student body had rarely seen. The sophomores, juniors, and seniors filed in to the bleachers under a dimmed light. The band stood to the side of the makeshift stage, trying not to show their hand. Once the bleachers were full, or nearly so, the gym went dark. That elicited hoots and hollers from a few of the guys who knew that the risk of yelling out in the dark and getting caught was minimal. At that moment, Taylor and the other band mates took the stage, positioned their instruments, then synchronized the opening note of their performance with the illumination of the gym. Following four clicks from Taylor's sticks, strobes began flashing all around, and the band strode into their opening song. I generally don't keep up with the modern trends in music, but from the reaction the group received, most in attendance were familiar with their opening number and greeted it with great enthusiasm. They went wild, to be honest, and Taylor just marveled at it all. You see, it had been some time since he had been in the spotlight, quite literally.

The concert, if you will, was laid out perfectly. It followed a similar format to that used by some of the ultramodern mega churches of today. You fire the crowd up with a few catchy numbers, then hit them with the message–and pass the plate. The guest preacher for this day's sermon was Taylor Ross.

When the band finished their second number, the lead singer grabbed the microphone and announced, "All right people, it's time to give it up for the founder of our feast, live from the rock group Vulture, a survivor of ol' Hamilton High, give it up for Taylor Rocks!"

The crowd cheered with enthusiasm, even though they had no idea who or what they were rooting for. I'm sure many of the kids had heard Vulture's music on the radio in the past and had probably spotted their albums in their parents' music collection, but for most, that's as far as their knowledge of Taylor and his group went.

I think he missed the spotlight, because when his name was announced, Taylor bounded up from his drummer's stool to the mic and waved. While there was no back flip, it was a lot like old times, I suppose, but on a much smaller scale. However, crowds are crowds, no matter what the size nor the age.

"What's up, Hamilton High?" he yelled out, causing a little bit of feedback in the speaker system. The students yelled back in response. "I'm sure you're wondering what we're all doing here today."

"Getting out of class!" yelled one student.

"Hell yeah, getting out of class," he returned, trying to be cool. The faculty, including Kaylee and Principal Dooley, grimaced at Taylor's use of inappropriate language in front of the student body.

"But aside from that, we're here to talk about music. Have you liked what you've heard so far?"

The crowd roared its approval.

"Well, there's more where that came from. How would you all like to jam like these dudes up here?"

The answer was nearly unanimous with their whoops and hollers.

"Then here's what we have for you today. You all know—well, maybe you don't—but anyway, I was in a rock band called Vulture for nearly twenty years."

Surprisingly, there were a few shouts of support. I don't know if those individuals knew of Vulture, but most likely, these were merely the shouts from students you hear at nearly every assembly who just like to yell out at every mention.

"Yeah, rock on. Well, do you know where I got my start?" he asked. Even though there were a few suggestions like, "The gutter!" and the like from the crowd, Taylor didn't allow them to finish. "Right here; right here at good old Hamilton High. That's right; I was in the school's marching band. From there I learned how to jam."

"Nerd!" came a shout from the crowd.

Taylor froze. "Oh yeah? Listen you smart-ass, get your butt down here and let's hear you play. Get down here and do something, anything, other than run your mouth!"

The silence was deafening. "Just as I figured. Well let me tell you all one thing," he said, while staring in the direction of the heckler, "before I was even allowed to graduate, I was in San Francisco playing in a rock group called Vulture, and shortly after that, we had a recording contract and were traveling all over the world. I did that because I aspired to do something other than just sitting around the house doing nothing. Use your time to better yourself. You'll have plenty of time to relax when you're becoming food for the worms."

There were shouts of approval.

His voice got louder. "You can't tell me that in a school of two thousand students, you can't put more than twenty-eight people on the field for a marching band. What the hell's your problem, man? It's my goal to put ten times that number on the field so we can be the biggest and best band in Ohio, not just in high school, but the best in the entire state. The hell with the Buckeyes. What do you say?"

Surprisingly there was a fair amount of applause and cheering from the stands. Taylor then realized that he had to keep his speech short and to the point or he'd risk losing the audience's interest. In a true preacher's style, he lit into them with his big finish, adding emphasis to the first word to grab the congregation's attention.

"*You* have that same opportunity to reach for the top. *You* can do it here today in music, or in anything you set your sights on. *You*," he said, again with emphasis, "can do what you want. It's up to you, folks, not the other clowns you hang with, not your parents, and not even your teachers."

Taylor began pacing from one side of the stage to the other.

"Guys, ten years from now, you probably won't even see ninety-five per cent of the other people sitting here in this gym. Look around. Look at the person next to you. You won't see most of these people again in your lives, so why are you so hell-bent on impressing them? What does their opinion matter anyway?" There was silence. All ears were open. He had them now.

"If you want to be a rocket scientist when you graduate from college, then I say go for it. But, if you want to be involved with your high school now, be in a really rad band, wear your school's colors with pride, and attend ten football games for free, then put aside your fears of trying something new, trying something that you once thought to be uncool, and for once in your life do something for yourself. Guys, I hate to be the bearer of bad tidings, but you only have one go-around in this life. Don't go to your graves saying, "Wow, I wish I had done a few more fun things in high school, but I was too uncomfortable with how people might view me." If you commit to this here, today, and anything else you set your sights on throughout your school years, I guarantee you'll do well in your life. If you don't mind being a bottom feeder, somebody who sits home all day on your ass exercising your thumbs on a Nintendo game; well then, there's certainly no shortage of people like that because doing that takes no effort. Don't waste your time playing computer games, design them. Don't just go to the game, be a part of it. If you want to better yourself today, and for the rest of your life, step forward and begin being your own person. Listen to your heart. Find out what you're made of." Taylor's voice then quieted. His message had been delivered. It was time for his speech's icing. "Guys, it's up to you. What do you want to do today? Are you willing to answer the call? What do you want to do with the rest of your life?"

The band then began playing very softly, much the same way a church organist would play when the preacher would segue from his sermon to the collection. Taylor handed the microphone back to the lead singer, then walked back to the drummer's stand. He pulled the sticks out of his back pocket, turned them over to the student drummer, then walked off to the side of the stage.

"Folks," began the vocalist, "Taylor will be in the band room right after seventh period. Stop on in and sign up. We want you. We need you."

With that, the band stopped its music entirely. The announcer took a deep breath and let loose with, "Go Blue! Beat the Middies!" The sticks clicked loudly together four times, but this time the resulting rhythm was faster and more deliberate.

Without skipping a beat, the band began a hard rock jam that had the crowd on its feet. The spotlights were circling, the band was jamming, and the crowd was cheering.

The assembly continued on for another twenty minutes, with one of the musical highlights occurring when the rock band struck their version of the Hamilton High Big Blue marching song. That song was a traditional march, but the band threw together their rock version of the song, and everyone thought it was pretty wild.

Introduction of the players and coaches was nearly anticlimactic, but a spirited pep speech by the coach saved the day and rounded out of the afternoon's festivities. When the assembly concluded, the stage was cleared, and students returned to their classrooms for final attendance. Taylor walked back to the music room to prepare for the throng of students that would be arriving to join the band.

Just as the final bell sounded, Kaylee walked in and picked up the ongoing dispute from where the two left off.

"You know, it would be nice if you let someone in on your little projects once in a while," she stated with emphasis on the last four words.

"Hey, I was hired to recruit new members, amongst other duties. I do what I have to do. If I waited for you to do your own thing, this band would be twenty-eight members for the next ten years."

"And where does it sit today?" She stood with arms crossed as she looked around the empty room. "Looks like twenty-eight members still. Oh, I'm sorry, twenty-six. I stand corrected. You never did convince the two members who quit to return, did you? And by the way, your potty-mouthed speech at today's assembly surely won't be overlooked by the powers that be. That's okay, though, because after those in charge get wind of your little escapades, you'll be out on your keister and our troubles will be over."

"Oh, you'll run the show all by yourself?"

"If I have to. Regardless, it looks like your little self-serving stunt didn't…"

Just then, the door swung open and six students walked in.

"Hey Taylor, you rock, man!"

Doing his best Elvis impression, Taylor struck a 'King-like' pose, and with his hands outstretched, said with a sneer on his lip, "Thank you, thank you very much."

"Man, you burned it up today."

"That I did. Not bad for an old man, huh? Now the question is, do all of you want to burn it up each Friday night and be famous as well? Are you ready to be the center of attention and entertain the crowds? Are you ready to join the band and answer your school's call?"

"Heck yeah," seemed to be the consensus. "With you as the leader, this ought to be a great time."

"It is a great time, but it is a lot of hard work as well. I'm not going to B.S. you. If you're willing to do the work, we'll get along just great. I'll tell you what, give Miss Lewis your information and what instrument you play, and we'll see about getting everyone suited up."

And that was a problem, for you see, Taylor was relatively successful in recruiting new members, but forgot that there were few spare uniforms to go around. They never needed them before.

"And what do you plan to do about that?" Kaylee asked. "You have thirty-two new members, and only thirty one uniforms-total! You've increased the size of the band, but we have no way on suiting these people up. As the old saying goes, your heart might have been in the right place, but your head was out to lunch."

"Oh, now you're quoting Shake-rear."

"Hey, we have a problem here, Einstein. We have neither the time nor the money to do this properly. Now do you want to know why I said to check with me first before pulling off one of these stunts?"

"Hey, I did my part. I got the people here. At least you could help out a little bit. Use your head for something other than a hat rack, and contribute a little something."

"Okay, fine, I'll come up with a solution to the uniform dilemma, but now I have to ask how you plan to integrate these new members into an existing band? Our formation positions are already set. These people have been practicing all summer on these numbers. We would have to totally revamp our formations and throw everything we've practiced out the window. Have you given any thought to that?"

"Simplicity, my dear. We don't have to do all of these fancy formations. The people want to hear the band play. They don't have to parade around all over the field. We'll concentrate on the music."

"Taylor, they're a *marching band*. They're supposed to parade all around, as you put it."

"Okay, we can work with that. We can just have them snug up their formations…"

"We?"

"Okay, I will then. But I still say that they don't have to march everywhere. They can form a tunnel when the team comes on the field, form a rectangle to play the school song, then march off. Problem solved, at least until half time."

"And what do you plan to do for that?"

"One thing at a time, my dear."

Well, the formation quandary took care of itself as they utilized Taylor's plan of simplicity. They got by, anyway. While they didn't look great, they sounded stronger, but then again, that wouldn't take much. As far as the uniform situation went, well, Kaylee came up with an innovative solution. The new members would wear black trousers and blue shirts. They would be interspersed with the existing uniformed members to give the band some semblance of consistency. That, too, worked. So even though Kaylee and Taylor were at each other's throats for the remainder of that month, they did manage to work together, whether they wanted to admit it or not. Not all was smooth sailing, though. Taylor had a way of drilling the kids over and over. He was trying to make up for lost time. That got to Kaylee. She was used to old Mr. Harmon saying over and over, "Good job, folks."

"Why do you drive these kids so hard? Perfection isn't all it's cracked up to be, especially at this level."

"And an attitude like that is what got this band in the sorry shape that it's in. Just good enough is, well, just good enough. If you don't sell out for your cause, what's the point? Why bother? Can't you envision these kids being better than average? Haven't you wanted to be better than average?"

"You occasionally bring up Mr. Harmon's name. You're just the opposite of him. Just listen to yourself sometime."

"Thank you."

Kaylee just glared at Taylor.

"Look, let's just settle this thing once and for all," Taylor began. "You don't like me, and I don't like you. To be honest, I don't need some teeny-bopper hanging around, sticking her nose in everything I do. Even with Vulture, I was a solo act most of the time. I wrote the songs, and with help from the guys, performed the songs. So why don't you just peddle your papers someplace else. I have the situation well in hand."

"You egotistical bastard! Is that what you think I am, some teeny-bopper? I'll have you know that I have my Master's Degree in education and have been teaching for six years now. The only inexperience here is you and your lame attempt to put an egg back into its shell. Tell you what, I'll let you mess things up on your own, and when you come crawling back, I'll laugh and tell you that I told you so."

With that, Kaylee got up and left the room. Taylor realized that he probably crossed the line, but in a position of authority, he felt more at ease being the antagonizer as opposed to playing second fiddle.

The season finished out with the football team sporting a respectable six and four record, and Taylor had fulfilled his obligation. Even with Kaylee off his back, Taylor's path was anything but smooth. Someone was spreading rumors that the high school had a druggie running the band. Taylor suspected that it was Bob Harmon, but he had no proof. Bob did have a motive, he also had access to school board members, and finally, he possessed a degree of time-tested credibility. While I wouldn't have put it past him, neither of us had any evidence to link the two.

In just a few short months, Taylor had gone from being a recluse, to person who found himself meeting with parents, and members of the student body as well. It was a painful process, being reborn into society, but Taylor had never failed in the business world, and he didn't intend on doing so now.

In the past, Taylor had spent the majority of his time touring with a rock band, and before that, as a student in school. Neither of those activities really contributed much to the social order, as he put it, but now he was focusing on something that made a difference in others' lives. He had taken a floundering band and doubled its size.

He had helped others appreciate music, and hopefully now they would carry that enjoyment over into their post-academic lives. But now that the season had come to an end, Taylor didn't know what to do with himself.

While he had rented a townhouse here in the city, I assumed that once the season was over, he would terminate his lease and head back to Los Angeles. In talking with him, though, he spoke of recruiting new members for the upcoming season, and maybe even getting a band bus. Those were lofty goals for someone with one foot out the door.

No one was more surprised to see Taylor hanging around than Kaylee. I think she was looking forward to getting her desk and office back, but Taylor showed up every day, pecked around on his laptop, and continued being a nuisance, at least in her eyes. She finally broke down and asked Taylor, "Why are you still hanging around here?"

"Hey, let me finish what I started."

"So I take it you're thinking of staying on as band director."

"I might. I told everyone that I could put a band on the field ten times the size of Harmon's. I plan to fulfill my pledge."

The tension wasn't what it could have been. Kaylee wasn't in her office very often at this point, as she was either in class most of the day, or in the teacher's lounge. Taylor came and went as he pleased. We grabbed lunch on occasion at the fast food joint across from the school, but mostly he went solo.

When his tenure at Hamilton began, Taylor went out and purchased a top-of-the-line laptop computer, and now spent much of his time on the internet researching marching bands, their

75

formations, and training techniques. To be honest, I think Kaylee felt sorry for him and let him be. Under those circumstances, those two coexisted about as well as could be expected.

One day, just before Thanksgiving break, Taylor was in the office the two shared, and they were working on their respective projects when a young African-American student named Jamaal Payton knocked on the door.

"Yes?" Kaylee asked.

"Um, I'm here to see Taylor-man," he answered.

Kaylee went back to her paperwork.

"What do you need, my friend?" Taylor asked.

"Um, my mom had this old album of yours and wanted to know if you could autograph it for her. Jamaal handed Taylor Vulture's inaugural album *Light of the Moon*.

"Well, heck yeah. I always have time for my fans. Do you like Vulture's music?

"Are you crazy? I ain't into that crap. All you sing about it wars and flowers and things. That stuff's too white for me. Not enough beat."

"I beg your pardon. I was the drummer in that band."

"Like I said."

Kaylee just snickered, an act that didn't go unnoticed by Taylor. He glanced her way for a split second, then turned his attention back to the task at hand. He dug out his pen and asked, "And you are?"

"Jamaal Payton."

"Who do you want it signed to?"

"Just sign your name, man. It don't matter."

"Fair enough." Taylor flipped the album around once or twice, then decided to sign it right across the moon on the cover.

"There you go, partner. Anything else?"

Jamaal just stood there for a moment and stared at the signature. "No, I guess not."

He was slow to leave, so Taylor suspected that Jamaal might be there for a reason other than an album signing.

"Um, Jamaal, do you play any instruments?"

Jamaal began laughing. "You're kidding, right? You think I want to join the band or something? You've got to be kidding. I'm only here because my mom wanted to see if you were dumb enough to sign this. Shoot, why would I want to hang with a bunch of band nerds for? Plus, I've played before larger crowds than what they have here at the football games, so that's no big thing. I don't need it. I don't need you," he said while pointing his finger in Taylor's direction.

"Oh, so you do play."

Jamaal panicked a bit. "Get lost, man." He turned and walked out. There was silence for a moment.

"So, you finally met your match, huh? You finally discovered that you can't convert the whole world," Kaylee said.

"He's not my match. He'll be back."

"Oh, you think so?"

"I know so. Did you see that price tag on the back of that album?"

"Yes. So?"

"It was a two dollar tag…from Vintage Records and Tapes over on Third Street."

"So? Two bucks? Sounds like you finally hit the big time."

"Vintage just opened up a month or two ago. If his mother asked him to obtain an autograph on her personal album, then her nostalgic streak doesn't run very deep. My guess is that he bought that record himself."

"You think?"

"I do."

"Then why did he buy it? Did he just want to meet you in person? He could have done that any time."

"He needed an excuse. He wanted to meet me and see if I was legit. He was sizing me up. The album signing was just a cover."

"Don't flatter yourself."

"I'm serious. Next, he'll check out the band and see if it's for real."

"We'll see."

The football season had been over for a month, and the marching band didn't participate in any post-season band competitions, not this year anyway. That wasn't unusual though. Bob Harmon wasn't big on those events either. Taylor was still around working his magic on his keyboard. This time, however, the keyboard belonged to a computer rather than a piano. Oh, he still did some work with individual band members interested in furthering their music careers. Taylor would also hold court in the band room every day after school. Even though he had no assigned tasks at that point, he was there regardless. He figured the more he could reach the students, the greater his chance of winning over the school populous.

"Word of mouth has sold more cars than all of the television ads combined," he used to say.

Taylor decided to implement my suggestion of trying to win the students over by relating his experiences from the 'old days' of playing on the road, and despite his skepticism, he did a pretty fair job. His 'court' grew appreciably with each passing day. Taylor finally realized that the sixties and early seventies were periods that will never be again, and the students, even those not interested in joining the band, were dying to hear this senior citizen tell of the days when he was roughly their age. Taylor figured that he didn't have anything to lose, so he did his best to keep it clean. That was a task in and of itself.

When Taylor began these 'fireside chats,' as I called them, he decided to begin at the top, then let the conversation work its way to the bottom. "That's how we all get to know one another," he said.

"Okay, first of all, when I went here to Hamilton High, my name was actually Ross Taylor."

"Why did you change it to Taylor Ross? Were you bored?"

"Good line…for a ten year old. No, actually I changed it because early on because while doing a concert in the park in San Fran, someone shouted from the crowd during one of my long, drawn out drum solos, "Taylor rocks!" Well, in my state, I thought someone was shouting 'Taylor Ross.' Later on, someone clued me in on the correct phrasing, so I kind of adopted it as my handle–Taylor Ross, Taylor Rocks. I had it legally changed a few years later…I think. It was the sixties you know, so I'm not real sure at this point. That's funny. Hmm."

Then there was the one day while holding a B.S. session with fifteen to twenty students, Taylor suddenly lost control of the meeting. No, nothing physical or major went on, but the students took over and became the talkers rather than the listeners. Apparently, several of the students boned up on their sixties and seventies rock-and-roll trivia, and decided to put Taylor to the test. I guess they wanted to see if he was the real deal. That was a good sign, for they were trying to see whether Taylor was worth trusting.

"Taylor, who was your favorite drummer…other than yourself?" The question brought the predicted laughter.

"Well, I've known all of the best. I knew Ian Paice. Do any of you know who he was?"

"He was with Deep Purple, wasn't he?"

"Very good. How about Stewart Copeland? Do any of you recall hearing his name?"

"The Police," shouted two or three students.

"Wow, how old are you folks?" There was laughter. "And of course the great Ginger Baker of Cream. Man, you talk about a diverse percussionist. And smooth…" he said while shaking his head from side to side.

"Who did you hang out with, I mean, other than the other 'lads'?"

"Lads. Don't get me started on those guys. But speaking of The Beatles, I actually liked Ringo. He certainly wasn't the best drummer in the land, but he was a bona fide success story. He only had a few years of real experience under his belt when he joined The Beatles, and his early stuff was basically all cymbal, but he eventually developed into a real fine drummer. He could carry a beat."

"So Ringo was your favorite?"

"Oh, hell no. I only met him once or twice, and bumped into him a handful of other times. Now Steven Tyler and me were buds. He wasn't a drummer, but we had some great times together."

"Partied hardy, huh?"

Taylor just smiled. "We had some good times together."

"What was your band like?

"We were a rag-tag thrown together bunch. We weren't a classic rock band, per se. We had a bit of an edge to our music. Starting out, I was the only one without any real big time experience. Rounding out the cast, there was Red…"

"And Sonny, Charlie Hodges, and the Colonel?" asked one of the class clowns.

"No, but like I told some of you a while back, I did meet Elvis. I didn't like him, mind you, and I don't think he liked us too much." They all laughed. "At that point of his career, he was no longer about the music. Elvis was about Elvis."

"Wow, did you hang out with him any?"

"No, not a lot. Those of us in Vulture didn't really fit in with The King and his court, if you know what I mean. I think Elvis thought we were bit too crude for his taste–a bunch of bangers, I think he once referred to us. And that, coming from a man who used to eat peanut butter and banana sandwiches."

"Eww," replied the one girl.

"I can only assume he believed that our blue jeans just didn't mix well with his blue suede shoes."

"Anyway, like I said, there was Red, or Ernie Huber, John Winston, or J. Dub as we used to call him, and I emphasize *used* to call him, God rest his soul."

"Did he die?"

"Yes, about ten to fifteen years ago. He originally came to us after doing some studio work with a British band called *The Magic Lanterns* back in the early to mid-sixties. He was considered the worldly one because he had traveled overseas to work with that group. Most of us felt lucky to be in San Francisco. I did see a lot of the country on the way out, though."

"You eventually spent some time in Great Britain, I take it?" asked Gordon, one of the more studious members of the woodwind section.

"Correct you are. You know, early on I used to envy John for his travels. Later, after Vulture became established, we all went over there, England that is, for the summer. Yep, in sixty-eight, The Beatles traveled to India, and to fill the void, we landed in jolly ol' England. Anyway, we met up with the members of a rock group called The Yardbirds while beginning our tour of Europe that summer. I don't know if any of you have heard of them or not. As it was, they were in the final days of their existence. They put out some pretty good music in their day though. Robert Plant was one of their lead singers. He went on to perform with Led Zeppelin. And that was a coincidence, because I guess you could say that we eventually became friendly rivals with Led Zep, even though that's about the only time we really got together. Anyway, The Yardbirds and the members of Vulture thought of cutting a single together in their studio one night, but I guess we were a bit too wasted for it to sound up to snuff. When you wake up and find someone else sleeping in your shoes, you begin to realize that it's time to tone it down a bit. Needless to say, we shelved that idea. Could you imagine if we'd pulled that one off though?"

"Do you miss John?"

"John? Well, I think of him occasionally, although not as much as I once did. Time has a way of doing that. John and I had our disagreements, God knows. But you know, I always felt a little sorry for him. He was basically a good guy, but I guess you could say that he collapsed under the weight of his own genius. You know, his brain was so heavily weighted on the creative side that it left little room for anything else, let alone common sense."

"What happened to him?"

"John got all messed up on heroin for a while. That destroyed his spirit within the band, not to mention himself, and that's when I took over and really made things take off for us. That caused some resentment around Vulture because I basically resurrected a floundering group, and some people began referring to us as Taylor Ross and his band. It was a team effort to be sure, but someone had to take charge, you know? But I guess it's true what they say; 'don't let a good deed go unpunished.'"

"Anyway, what got John clean was that one time when he went to cook up some of his stuff in a spoon, he was so messed up that that he didn't realize that he had picked up a plastic picnic spoon.

Well, it caught fire and ended up dripping that hot melted plastic on his hand and leg. Not being in his right mind, I guess he thought the melting spoon was just a manifestation of his warped mind, until he noticed that his pants leg was on fire. Once he finally calmed down and got his stuff together, he figured that he probably looked the part of a fool and ended up with a pretty burned hand and leg to boot. He was really messed up. He was never able to play again as I recall. That must have scared him straight because after a stint in the hospital to treat his burns, he was actually clean as a whistle for the last handful of years of his life as far as I know. His wild life took its toll on him, and in the end, he passed due to the weight of the excesses in his life."

"Is that how you remember him, a heroin addict?"

"Oh hell, no. John was the king of the double-necked guitar. I used to laugh at that instrument saying that John was just too lazy to play a standard six string the way it was supposed to be played, so he added a neck and tuned it differently to hit those difficult notes easier. It had nothing to do with the production of a different sound, even though that was the true intention of that innovation. I remember him for all of his quirks."

"What about the rest of your members? Are they all dead too?"

"Not as far as I know. Red Huber is still around, I think. He was basically a studio musician, so maybe that's what he's still doing. Pops Dixon, the oldest amongst us, played in several bands before naming us The Screeching Vultures, as we were known for about one gig, then just Vulture. We sucked as the Screeching Vultures and figured that it had to be our name that caused our poor performance." The students all laughed.

"Pops was our Mick Jagger, if you will; strictly vocals. I think his guitar was more for show than anything else. Finally, there was our bassist 'Clueless' Joe Paxton. We always used to say, 'He must have been clueless, otherwise he would have ended up a musician rather than a bassist.'"

"So you all had nicknames?"

"Well of course."

"What was yours?"

"Like I said, I was Taylor Rocks."

"Did you hook up with any of the roadies?"

Taylor just stared at the girl. "Um, I think you mean 'groupies.' The roadies were the dudes who set up our stage." Everyone began to laugh. "The answer is no."

"Okay," she yelled above the laughter, "groupies then. Did you ever hook up with any of them?"

"What kind of question is that?"

"An honest one."

"And a personal one as well. They were around. I mean," he said, trying to find a delicate way of explaining something that wasn't anyone else's business, "you know, I mean, if that's what you were looking for, well, then it was there. Not me, however," he said with his hand across his heart in a demonstration of his mock sincerity. "I was an angel."

"Not even a special someone?" asked Courtney, a junior flutist.

Taylor sat for a moment. No one said a thing, for they were waiting to hear what he was about to divulge. Their anticipation was rewarded.

"Anyone of you heard of a singer named Janis Joplin?"

"Wow," was the buzz around the room. "You dated her?"

"Yeah, a little bit, but nothing earth-shattering to speak of there."

"She was wild, from what I've heard. Were you two lovers?" That question brought a roar from the students.

"Courtney!" shouted one of the other girls from the back.

"Well, you don't know unless you ask."

"It's none of your business. Anyway, it's getting late. It's time for me to head out, and for all of you all to scoot. See you all tomorrow."

Taylor bailed, more-so because he was covering up the fact that there *was* more to the Janis Joplin story than he was willing to divulge. You see, though contacts, Taylor got to know Chuck Jones, the drummer for Big Brother and the Holding Company. Big Brother was Janis Joplin's band at that time. Anyway, Chuck introduced Taylor to Janis, and he was smitten right away. There was an age difference between the two, as he was barely twenty while she was a 'mature' twenty-six. That was a pretty wide gap considering that she was so much worldlier than most people at that age. And she had become an old pro within the business, not to mention that she was quite seasoned as far as her love life went. In comparison, Taylor had barely scratched the surface.

By that time, Joplin, it was rumored, was addicted to heroin, allegedly shooting at least two hundred dollar's worth of the stuff every day. Taylor was no match for that. Oh, he thought he knew more than he actually did and tried to keep up, but in reality, Taylor was little more than a 'plaything' for Ms. Joplin. I'm not sure what he initially hoped to accomplish with her. Maybe he was looking for a mother figure. But through it all, a good time was a good time.

Unfortunately for Taylor, this was only the beginning of his fascination with achieving the unobtainable when it came to his love relationships. After his experience with his mother, and the way she returned little in the way of love and affection during his formative years, Taylor just couldn't see settling for anything but the best. He had paid the price, he once said.

As football season became a distant memory, and shortly thereafter replaced by hoops, I suggested that Taylor and I take in a game. Like football, it had been decades since Taylor had attended a basketball game.

It was a full house, as the Big Blue rarely had trouble attracting fans. There was a long-standing winning tradition for the home team, one that even trumped football.

As we entered the gymnasium, the memories came flooding back to me, as it was déjà vu all over again, as the old saying goes. It seemed like only yesterday that Taylor and I walked through the same double doors on a given Friday night. The cheers had been updated a bit, but they conveyed a similar message; massacre the opponent, but in a sportsman-like way. It was a flashback to yesteryear, as one couldn't help but notice that the identical humid, sweat-sock aroma from years gone by still filled the air, and I noted that modern day basketball shoes still made that high-pitched chirp, identical to their latter day counterparts. Back in the day, Taylor and I would worm our way up towards the top of the bleachers, yell at our friends to join us, then make plans for after the game. Rarely were those plans aboveboard, if I recall correctly. Such is the life of a sixties high schooler with access to 3.2 beer.

Some things never change, I mused, as Taylor and I made our way up through the clutter of aisle-littering legs, sneakers, and handbags in search of a couple of seats three-fourths of the way up the bleachers.

The fifteen or so band members played their background music as the two teams warmed up, then they got a bit racy, at least for a high school band. They struck up the theme song for Budweiser Beer to the delight of the student body.

"How the hell are they getting away with that?" Taylor asked. "I know it's been a while, but I find it difficult to believe that a teacher would allow their band to even practice that. Who runs the pep band here anyway?"

"No one."

"No one? I beg your pardon."

"No one. They're not an official school-sponsored band. These guys have thrown together their own student-run band for over ten years. After a school levy failed back in the mid-nineties, one of the things they eliminated was the pep band leader. I believe the man's name was Gustafson or something like that. Anyway, the game seemed to be lacking something, so a group of students got together and formed their own band. I remember their battle cry was something like, 'We don't need no stinkin' leader,' sounding reminiscent of the often misquoted line from *The Treasure of the Sierra Madre*. They do a pretty good job though."

"Darned right they do. I'm going to speak with them at halftime."

"They'll blow you off. They like their autonomy."

Well, the half rolled around with Hamilton up by eight, and after the band finished their two spirited numbers, they got up to leave. Taylor intercepted them at the bottom of the bleachers and followed them out into the hallway.

"Hey guys, Taylor Ross," he said while extending his hand.

"Yeah, we know who you are. We were at the assembly a while back. You're pretty good."

"*Pretty* good?"

"Yeah. Your beat is a bit antiquated, if I may say," remarked one of the members.

"Well, be that as it may, I was hoping that I could interest you all in joining the marching band.

"Naw," came the answer in unison.

"Oh come on, guys. You all are pretty darn good. Put some structure in your music. After high school, you'll be able to earn a little money with it."

"I already do," remarked the drummer.

"Well there you go. The rest of you could do the same thing. Maybe even get a music scholarship." The mob still wasn't convinced. "A scholarship beats having to go out and work a job for money, take out a tuition loan, or beg your parents to foot the bill." That turned a few heads. There was a silence.

"Maybe. You'll guarantee me a scholarship?"

"I can't guarantee you that. Neither can anyone else. But this is the only path to those means. Plus, with your experience, you might be able to show those with less musical knowledge how it's done. How about it?"

"Maybe. When do you have to know?"

"No particular time. We begin practice in earnest right after school lets out in early June. Until then, feel free to drop by the music room. I'll be there."

Taylor felt as if he had made some excellent headway in attracting some new talent to the band. He knew he still had a long way to go if he intended to hit his goal. He also knew it would take time. He wasn't sure how much of that he had left.

It was mid-November, and when he was occupying his little corner of the office, Kaylee walked in.

"Hey man, I think I managed to get most of the folks from the basketball pep band to consider joining the marching band. That's something."

"That's cool. That will certainly help the cause. So you're staying, I take it."

"I beg your pardon?"

"I take it you're staying. You're still here and the season is long over. You're still recruiting."

"I made a promise to these kids. I intend to give it my best shot."

"I see. So, what do you have going on for the holidays? Will you be heading back home to California?"

Well, I don't really have a home there. I have a house, but no family to speak of. I'll probably just hang around here."

"No family? None?"

"Nope. The term 'family' to me refers to a God-created spiritual experiment that went bad."

"Oh, that's terrible to think about the cornerstone of civilization that way."

"The headstone, you mean."

"Okay, let me ask you; without family, where would we be? Where would you be?"

"A hell of a lot better off, as far as I'm concerned."

"That's shocking to hear you say that. You're obviously a very bitter man."

"Oh, you think? Walk a mile in my shoes, lady."

"You're heading towards sixty years old, for God's sake. That resentment you're feeling has to be getting a bit old. Haven't you ever heard of forgiveness? God forgives sins far greater than a botched childhood."

"I'm not God. I actually thought about running for the position until I found out it had already been filled. I am who I am."

"Such a sarcastic idiot."

"Thank-you. Where the hell are you heading for the holidays, the Walton's?"

"Pretty close. I have some relatives in New England that I've been meaning to see. I've been asked to head up there."

"I'll probably just hang around the apartment, catch up on my reading, surf the net and the like."

"I see. I'm really looking forward to visiting New England this year. I'd like to be there when it snows. It's supposed to, and I've never experienced a white Thanksgiving before, but…"

"But?"

"You know, I've always wanted to bake a turkey in my own place, but those things are so darn big that I'd have so much left over."

"Uh huh."

Kaylee looked a bit agitated. Something was troubling her. She shifted in her chair, then took a deep breath. "Um Taylor–oh boy, I'm really going out on a limb here," she said with a big sigh. "Um, would you like to come over to my place for Thanksgiving dinner?"

"You're kidding, right?"

"No, it's a legitimate offer. You could watch the game on television…"

"I don't really get into football. I barely tolerate it when I'm running the band on Friday night."

"Okay then, I could record the Rose Bowl parade, or whatever. That way, you could criticize the bands."

The Rose Bowl parade is on New Year's. You're thinking of the Macy's Thanksgiving Day Parade."

"Whatever! Is it a date?"

"A date?"

"Poor choice of words. Do you want to come to dinner or not?"

"Man, you must be pretty desperate to ask me."

"Okay look, forget it."

"Hell no, I'm not going to forget it. You offered and I accept. I'll be there. What time?"

After a long look, she replied, "How about five-thirty?"

"I'll be there or be square."

"Oh, why do I think this is going to be a disaster?" Kaylee asked out loud. Taylor just laughed.

"You're stuck with me now, chickey-poo!"

After that meeting, Taylor went home to his dark apartment. The closer it got to the holidays, the earlier the sun faded from view. That's just the way it is. Heading towards one of the most enjoyable and celebrated times of year can also be one of the most depressing times of year with the darkness and cold settling in all around.

It was a little after five o'clock when Taylor arrived home. He entered the living room, took a seat on the couch, and began staring at nothing in particular. I think that the depressing part of the season was making its presence felt. It was dark, cold, and Taylor did little with his time other than work; he always worked. In the past, he was used to the warmer Southern California weather, even at this time of year, and spending his day lounging around his Rockwood estate, as he called it.

There was only one light on, the one in the foyer, and Taylor had yet to switch on the end table light. He gave a fleeting glance at the newspaper, but giving it a serious read proved to be too much of a task under the given circumstances. He glimpsed over at the clock, then, as if inspired, reached over and picked up the phone. He dialed ten digits, then waited for an answer. He received one, and he knew he would, because even at the local hour, California was three hours behind us.

"Yeah, Jerry. Taylor Ross. Yeah, it has been a long time. Me, just hanging out. Yeah, I'm feeling a lot better too. Thanks. Yep, clear as a bell. Not bad for an old man. Yeah, I know there's no work. I'm not calling about that. I need a favor. I need you to check on the house for me. Yes, I'll pay you, for God's sake–usual rate. I'm out in Ohio right now and might be for some time."

"What, you're staying in Ohio? What the hell for? Do you have family there or something?" he asked.

"Yep, family, you could say that."

Chapter 4

**Celebrate Me Home**

*"A good composer is slowly discovered;*

*a bad composer is slowly found out."*

~ Ernest Newman

Taylor showed up at Kaylee's house right at five-thirty, and in doing so, it appeared to her that he didn't want to spend one more second in the same room with her than was absolutely necessary. That wasn't true. He didn't believe in showing up fashionably late, but he also didn't think it was proper to arrive before his expected time either. So, he was always on time. That was just his way. In fact, he wasn't trying to avoid her company at all, but was just as nervous about this meeting as she was.

Taylor did his best to dress up for the occasion, but he hadn't brought many winter clothes with him when he left California. His jeans were fine, he thought, but his shirt was a little plain, a button-down, but that's all he had.

Kaylee greeted him at the door, and with the exception of her apron, she was dressed in a bit more formal attire.

"Hi. Come on in. I'm just getting the turkey out of the oven. Have a seat." Kaylee then ran off to the kitchen while Taylor looked around. The living room was smartly decorated, clean, and nicely lit. It wasn't as ritzy as his house in Beverly Hills, he thought, but far nicer than his townhouse.

As he walked around, the humid aroma of perfectly-prepared turkey, steaming peas, and boiling potatoes enveloped him. This must be what a real home smells like, he thought. He could grow attached to these smells, to a real home. It had been such a long time.

"Do you need help with anything?" he shouted to her in the other room.

"No, I'm fine. Just have a seat and I'll be there in a sec."

Taylor located an overstuffed chair that seemed to fit him and his mood at the moment, plopped down, and twiddled his thumbs while watching Kaylee setting all of the dishes on the table in the adjacent dining area. She has gone to an awful lot of trouble, he thought.

Kaylee continued to place plate after plate of steaming hot vegetables and turkey on the table, chatting the entire time.

"Well, we don't have snow like they're getting in New Hampshire, but it's still cold out. I like Thanksgiving. It's the kickoff to the Christmas season, and I simply love Christmas. I always have. Do you celebrate Christmas when you're in California?"

"No, not really."

Kaylee placed the last dish on the corner of the very crowded table, looked everything over, then pronounced it set. She called Taylor to the table. They both took a seat.

"Do you want to say the blessing?"

"Blessing? When I was little, my dad said that religion was for the weak, for those who needed a crutch of some sort. So I just…I'm really not into that kind of thing."

"Fine. Don't spoil this dinner with your anti-religious, holier-than-thou attitude. Can't you give it a rest for one evening and just enjoy the moment?"

"Whatever."

Kaylee stared at Taylor for a moment, then bowed her head. "Lord, we thank you for the food on this table and the company," she said, hesitating ever so slightly after that last word, "we are able to enjoy on this feast of Thanksgiving. Amen."

Taylor barely looked down during the prayer. When Kaylee looked up, Taylor asked, "Okay?"

"Yes, go ahead."

The two began taking a portion from each serving dish until the half dozen or so plates had made their rounds. Without saying much, Taylor began eating. Kaylee wasn't sure what to make of Taylor's silence, but she realized that it might have been ages since he had enjoyed a home-cooked meal of this caliber, so she tried not to take personally the quiet he exuded like a dark cloud. Still, she tried to pry a personality out of him.

"How's your turkey?"

"Good," Taylor answered between bites of stuffing.

"You haven't even tried it yet."

"Then why did you ask?"

"Why did you answer? And while I'm at it, why do you always have to be so damned defensive? Why are you so pissed at everyone and everything in your life?"

"Walk a mile in my shoes, missy."

"What's that supposed to mean?"

"You probably think that, just because I was someone at some point in time, I have no problems. Let me tell you, money isn't the answer to everything."

"I didn't say it was, but you have this massive chip on your shoulder, especially towards me. What did I ever do to you?"

"You wouldn't understand."

"I wouldn't understand what? That you're no longer a rock star, no longer recognized on the street? That you're getting older? Try me."

Taylor took another couple of bites knowing full well that Kaylee was staring at him the entire time awaiting his answer. He finally slammed his fork down and looked up. "What?!"

"Speak. Spill your guts. I'm sick and tired of your pissy-assed attitude towards everything–so open up!"

Taylor forcefully shoved his plate back. "Just make me a plate and I'll be on my way. I don't need this."

"No."

"What do you mean, no?"

"I mean, I went to a lot of trouble preparing this meal for you, and you walk in here and treat me like shit! I don't deserve that! You're not getting out of here until you tell me what your problem is. Do you have this enormous attitude because you're getting older and aren't the young, hip rock star you once were?"

Taylor just looked at her in disgust as if to say, "You're not even close, lady."

"Then why did you accept my invitation for dinner if you hate me so much?"

"I don't hate you."

"You sure as hell don't like me. I fix you a nice dinner and all, and you have nothing nice to say to me."

"I'm sorry. I wasn't aware that I was being difficult, but you must be right. I'm sorry."

He sat there silently for a spell. Finally, thinking that there had to be more to Taylor's acceptance of her invitation, Kaylee spoke up. "So?"

"So, I don't know… Maybe I felt sorry for you because you were all alone for the holiday."

"What? You…" Kaylee was beside her self at this point. "So you thought you'd brighten my day by keeping me company, your surliness adding sparkle to my otherwise dreary holiday? Are you for real? I ought to kick your sorry ass out of my house right now. You have a hell of a lot of nerve, buster!"

Kaylee rose from her chair, and in a fit of anger, slammed a lock of her hair behind her ear. "Do you want to hear the truth? I was the one who felt sorry for you!" Taylor wasn't totally surprised at her statement, but he patiently waited for an explanation.

"I could have traveled to join my family, but no, I chose to stay here thinking that if I didn't, you would have nothing to do but sit around your apartment and smoke your dope, or whatever the hell you do. I was trying to be a Good Samaritan, a good friend, and look where it got me!"

As Kaylee got up hastily to clear the table, a remorseful Taylor said in a low voice, "I'm sorry. You're right."

Kaylee stopped what she was doing and made her way to where Taylor was seated. "About?"

"About everything. I'm sorry," he said. He took a long, shaky breath. "I haven't had too much human contact in the last dozen years or so. I guess I've forgotten how to interact with people very well."

Kaylee set the plates down, placed her hands on her hips, and waited for Taylor to continue. She was certain more was to come.

"You're the only one who has taken the time to work with me on any project. In the early years, I was used to following somebody else's lead. In my later years, I was the creative leader and others followed me. I'm not real sure how to play the middleman. I don't…" He took another deep breath, then continued in a rapid-fire, almost panicky voice. "I have no idea how to communicate with these kids. That's your department. You're a teacher. You deal with them every day. I'm totally lost. I try, but my only experience with kids has been pumping out records and collecting the profits when they buy them."

"Taylor, what you're now selling isn't something the students can buy and then discard when they're done playing with it. You're selling inspiration, an ideal to which to aspire. Pass on your life's experiences. Win them over with new ideas, motivation, and encouragement."

"I'm trying. I'm doing the best I can. I-I tell them stories, and they laugh. I'm really not teaching them anything about band per se. I'm a joke to them, I suppose. I'm a lost soul from a bygone era. To them, I'm probably a freak from the past, an old hippie. That's

100

why...I wanted to ask you...um...if you could help me with that. I-I just can't do it myself."

Kaylee was stunned at Taylor's personal revelation.

Taylor lowered his head and teared up, for it wasn't in his psychological make-up to admit he wasn't master over his domain. Taylor rested his forehead on the palm of his hand.

Being sympathetic to his cause, Kaylee kneeled down at a still-seated Taylor and said, "Taylor, haven't you ever dealt with young people on a one-on-one basis at all before?"

"No," he said in a barely perceptible, phlegm-filled volume.

"No? Well, then this is really going to take you out of your element, you know."

"I know."

"Don't you have any younger brothers or sisters, maybe nieces or nephews? Can I be so bold to ask if you have any children of your own?"

Taylor took a deep breath. He hadn't looked up for some time. After a prolonged silence, he slowly parted his lips and said, "I don't think so, but after my gig on Letterman last year, a few of us in the band decided to go out and grab a bite to eat. There was one man in his mid-twenties, one of the studio musicians, who walked with us, seemingly ignoring all others in favor of me. He introduced himself as Justin Neumann. I shook his hand." Taylor's voice trailed off, then he took a moment to compose himself followed by an audible swallow. He was inadvertently twisting his napkin into a knot.

"As we headed to the limo, he muttered something about being my kid or something like that. Imagine that, my kid," Taylor said followed by a feigned laugh. "I get that crap all of the time, you know. Who the hell did he…think…" his voice trailed off. "He mentioned Lisa, my ex-old lady, as being his mother. Sheesh."

"How would he know your ex's name if he wasn't her son?"

"Hell, he probably Googled my bio or something like that, you know. Groupies. I told him to get lost."

"Is it possible? I mean, was she pregnant at any time in your relationship?"

"She took off in the middle of the night and got a quickie divorce–no alimony, no support, no nothing. I guess she was tired of all of my partying ways and just wanted out. I never saw her again after that night."

"Taylor, did he look like her?"

"I don't know. Maybe."

In a quiet, slow, non-accusatory tone, Kaylee asked, "Did he look like you?"

Taylor just bowed his head and nodded twice in the affirmative, then broke down and began sobbing. It was the first time he had displayed any great emotion in front of her, or anyone for that matter, since he had arrived home. This was a turning point in their relationship. This was a turning point in Taylor's life.

"Oh God." Kaylee put her arms around Taylor and just held him as he sobbed. A bond had been formed.

After a moment, he regained his composure and patted each eye with what was left with his napkin.

"Taylor, of course I will help you with the band. I just need a little cooperation from you, just a little," Kaylee said as she demonstrated by holding her thumb and index finger about a half inch apart. "Together we can pull this thing off."

"You think? Hell, I've been at it forever…"

"You've been at it for two months."

"Okay, two months, but I've barely scratched the surface. I mean, we're going to lose a lot of students through graduation. Somehow, I, uh, *we* have to field two hundred and eighty band members from nothing. How many do we have right now? Seventy?"

"Approximately. Why two hundred and eighty?

Taylor looked back down at the floor. "Because, when I got in the argument with Harmon, I told that bastard I could put together a band ten times the size of the one he fielded."

"Well, let's not concern ourselves with numbers right now. To paraphrase a famous movie quote, if we build it, they will come. If we make it the thing to do, the movement will attract more and more people. Nobody likes to be left out when a popular movement pops up, and it will seem like everybody is doing it except you. Nobody wants to be on the outside looking in."

"I suppose so. But how do we…I mean, where are we going to get all of these people to suddenly become musically inclined and want to take the field? If some people start taking lessons now, maybe they'll be qualified when the football season begins, maybe, but that's still only a small percentage. Where…" Taylor said, without finishing his sentence. "Oh God, what am I doing here? What have I done?"

"Look, there are a lot of possibilities we can explore. Let's get creative. We can send notes home to the parents. Those students who can play an instrument, well, their parents might be able to persuade them to join. It beats having them hang around the house all summer. There's also another avenue I've been thinking of."

"What's that?"

"There's a great untapped source of information that you haven't considered. We, at least I, have access to the students' files. I can look up those who were in band back in elementary and junior high school. You can check the yearbooks and make a list. I can check that list to the current records. It shouldn't be too hard for some of those people to pick it back up and do the cool thing."

"I never thought of that. Still, it would have to be a monumental sales job on our part. The kids think of me as an oddity at best right now. They'll never listen to me. You'll end up doing all of the work."

"We can fix that."

"How so?"

"Well, now don't get angry with me at what I'm going to suggest, but I think it's time for you to get a haircut."

"Not you too?"

"Taylor, you wanted suggestions. How bad do you want to accomplish your goal? If it's true that everyone around town says that you're just an old hippie, well, it might help your effort a bit if you came across to those in the community as one of their own instead of some leftist from a by-gone era."

Taylor took a deep breath. "I suppose so. Aw hell, do you know how long it's been since I've had a proper haircut?"

"Probably a generation or so, I'm guessing."

"I wonder if John still has his barber shop down on East Avenue? Hell, he would be about eighty years old now if he did. I don't want some shaky old hand trying to clean me up."

"Don't despair. I will do it."

"You? Up until a half hour ago, you were ready to dump the gravy boat in my lap."

"True, but while I was attending college, I worked as a beautician in my mother's shop. I did a pretty good job if I must say so myself. The tips were healthy."

"You were so good at it that you quit there to become a teacher?"

"Teaching was my major. Plus, it paid better. The benefits are nothing to sneeze at as well."

Taylor sat there for a moment, then looked up at Kaylee. She didn't flinch. She was being honest, and serious. Taylor shrugged. "Okay, have at it, Aphrodite."

Kaylee went over to the cabinet to retrieve her scissors and comb, then Taylor's statement hit her. She turned. "Who?"

"Wasn't she the Biblical chick who cut off the dude's hair and he lost all of his strength?"

"Hon, I think you mean Delilah–Sampson and Delilah."

"Oh. Who was Aphrodite then?"

"If I remember my Greek mythology, Aphrodite was a goddess that was born from the sea after one of the gods was castrated and his genitals were cast into the ocean," she replied with her eyebrows cast high.

"Oh good God, don't do that! Hey, stay away from me with those scissors!"

Both heartily laughed.

"I'm so embarrassed. I try to act like I'm educated, but I guess I'm not. I didn't even graduate from high school."

"Oh, I think you're smart. There's book smart, then there's people smart. You're people smart. You have to be, and that will carry you a long way towards reaching your goals in life."

"Well, okay. Do what you're going to do, but for God's sake don't mess with me and give me some dopey Dorothy Hamill wedge cut or something mean like that, for laughs."

"Don't worry, I do good...Dorothy Hamill? Boy, you are trapped in the past."

Kaylee secured a towel around Taylor's neck and performed her magic on his mane. When I say 'magic,' I'm not exaggerating. He was a bit of a mess. When she had completed her work, Taylor looked like a respectable, mature gentleman. He looked in the mirror and couldn't believe his eyes. Later on, people around town began referring to Taylor as 'Mr. Ross.'

"Wow, you really did a number on me. This is how I would have looked if I hadn't gone into rock. I look more like a CEO than a musician."

"You like?"

"Well, at this point in my life, with all that I've gone through, I guess I don't look half bad," he said rather matter-of-factly. "I think in another life you could have been a great artist because today you turned a lump of clay into something that is worthy of respect." Taylor then turned to Kaylee and said, "Listen up, because this may be the only time you'll hear this from me. Thank you."

"Well, I hope to hear it more often. After all, we are going to be working together as a team for a while, aren't we?"

"I guess we are."

"Okay, Monday I will gather up junior high yearbooks from the last three years, and you can list all of the band members' names. I'll look through the school records, then we can compare lists. There will be some duplicates I'm sure, but hopefully we can make some progress."

"Now that I have my new look, how about if I schedule meetings over at the junior highs to help in recruiting new members?"

"That would work. But wait–what are you going to talk about? You yourself said that you were no good with the kids."

"Right. Hmm, well I guess I can...that does present a problem. I can't let you shoulder all of the burden by yourself. That's not the point. I got us into this mess." Then it hit him. "I've got it! How about if I get the band together, the one we used at the assembly, and take our show on the road?"

"Now you're starting to sound like Mickey Rooney and Judy Garland. 'I know, let's put on a show!'"

"Now who's old? But you know, it could work. As they always say, you can get more flies with sugar than with salsa."

"Salt, I think you mean salt. You've been out in California too long. Anyway, it's worth a try. Monday, approach the band members and see if they can get free, and if their parents will give them permission. I'm sure they're going to hate missing school. Right. If that's a go, we'll contact the junior high principals and see what they think. That's a plan."

"How ironic that you said that. I've always said that you must have a plan in life. That's how I got as far as I did in the music world."

"Fine, Monday."

"Well…" Taylor said as a sign that there was nothing left to say and he was getting ready to leave.

"Um Taylor, before you go, I also have to ask you, did you put up a Christmas tree out at your place in California?"

"Hardly. I think I have one of those little Charlie Brown trees that some girl gave me years ago in a closet somewhere."

"Okay then, as this is a night of firsts, I'm going to go out on another limb and ask you what you have going on tomorrow?"

"I suppose I'm free. Why?"

"I would like to go and pick up a real Christmas tree, and I need a hand."

"A Christmas tree? It's only Thanksgiving. It would be as brittle as kindling by the time Christmas rolled around."

"I don't want to put it up tomorrow. I just want to pick it up."

"Wow, I can't remember the last time I was around a real Christmas tree. I guess it was when I was a kid. Ah, the smell of fresh cut pine and the soft boughs. There's a song in that somewhere."

"It's already been done, many times over."

"Yes, but that's what the holiday is all about."

"Well, it's about other things as well, but if you help me pick it up, you're welcome to share my Scotch pine any time. Tomorrow when we pick it up, we can put it on the back porch in a bucket of water. That way, it will stay fresh until we're ready to put it up. Plus, we'll get the best selection."

"We? That's plan, I guess." Taylor looked a bit sheepish now that it was time for him to go home. He really didn't want to leave, but he figured with fatigue setting in, he might say or do something that would upset the ceasefire the two had forged on that evening.

"Well, I'm going to head out and shower down and get all of these stray hair clippings off of me. I'm beginning to itch."

"You go and get your rest. I'll see you tomorrow around twelve. Is that okay?"

"That will work." Taylor didn't know whether to hug her goodbye, kiss her on the cheek, or just call it a night. To be safe, he performed the latter.


Taylor did indeed show up at Kaylee's place a little after noon on 'Black Friday.' Of course, everybody and their brother were out on the first official shopping day of the Christmas season. Taylor and Kaylee had it easy on this crazy afternoon, though, as they didn't plan to venture far from home, and they made it a point to avoid the malls. Few of those shopping centers carried cut trees anyway, but I'm sure they had a surplus of the plastic ones that came in a box.

The two were unsuccessful on their first three attempts. The first place only had a few trees out, as it was still early in the season. The second carried trees that, according to Taylor, looked as if they had been run over by the truck that delivered them, and the final place carried a supply of trees that were either lacking adequate branches or possessed a trunk that resembled the letter 'S'.

"I know. Let's drive out to Venice and cut our own."

"Won't we get in trouble?"

"No silly, we'll go to a nursery. They're a little bit more expensive, but you usually get what you're looking for."

"Cut our own? I suppose it's worth a try. This early stuff is a new experience for me. When I was a boy, Dad would always wait until the week of Christmas, for whatever reason, to begin shopping for a tree. Sometimes we would have to settle for pot-luck. We would always head across town and pick up a tree next to the Plaza, but I think there's a pizza joint there now."

The two drove out to the country nursery and exited the car into the pre-winter chill. The lightly-frozen gravel in the parking area gave way under their feet, popping and crunching gently, as the two ventured into the unexplored world of 'you cut-em' trees. The only sound to grace their ears, other than the frozen tundra beneath them, was the cheap horn speaker hastily mounted on the corner of a shed trying its damnedest to belt out a Christmas tune. The tinny sound was reminiscent of an old Victrola, but it got the job done.

To the side of the parking area, discarded pine boughs were popping and burning in a barrel in hopes of giving shoppers the scent of a colonial atmosphere, and yet at the same time disposing of the farm's refuse. Hot cider was available, at a greatly inflated price, as was hot chocolate. Christmas cookies and fudge were available inside the barn, but they were packaged up for take-home rather than for onsite consumption.

Despite being on the grounds of a one hundred and twenty-year-old farm, the axe had been replaced by a bow saw, and the trail through the woods now consisted of a path between neatly planted rows of trees that had been painstakingly sculpted and segregated according to type, size, and cost.

I don't know why, but with few exceptions, it always seems as if a cold Nor'easter blows in right after Thanksgiving Day around here giving those in the retail industry an excuse for a weak day, or on the flipside, a reason for their robust sales. It didn't matter. It was as if the shopkeepers were eager to point to an outside force as the reason for their bust or boom.

Taylor and Kaylee greeted the sales person at the entrance of the field, and he pointed them in the direction of the Scotch pines. To be on the safe side, he gave them a manual bow saw rather than risk the loss of limb with a chain saw.

The two strolled through the rows of Scotch pines, Norways, Blue Spruces, and White pines, hoping to find something befitting the holiday. They passed up row after row of candidates. It was as if they were looking for the perfect tree for the perfect Christmas. You see, while each of them were playing dumb at this point, both knew in their hearts that there was something special stirring between them. It was just a spark at this point of course, but in dry surroundings, that ember could ignite and take over the landscape. Both knew that.

"You know, now that I think of it, I do have a nice Christmas memory," Taylor said while looking out over the countryside.

"Really? I'd like to hear about that."

"When I was a little boy, my dad took me downtown around Christmas to see all of the shops decorated up and the like. Actually, I think he was going to pick up a gift for my mom at Wilmurs. I know you didn't grow up around here, but that was a time when there were so many little shops and department stores downtown. The area was bustling with activity. Anyway, on that night it was spitting a little bit of snow, and I remember there was a huge iron kettle set up on High Street in front of one of the banks, with a set of wobbly wooden stairs next to it so you could walk up and toss in a donation. It was so big that I believe they had to block off one lane of traffic to accommodate it. I'm guessing it was for the Salvation Army. My dad gave me two quarters, and I ran up the stairs and looked in. There was all sorts of money in there, and at the time I thought maybe the way they gave the money away was to have all of the needy people climb in and grab a handful or two. Merry Christmas, you know?"

"That's funny."

"Then, we walked a few blocks down towards the Soldiers and Sailors Monument, and next to it was a glassed-in stage with all of these automated figures in a Christmas scene. It was pretty dark on that street corner, but the enclosed stage was all lit up, and the colors...oh, the reds were redder than any I had ever seen. There were greens, silver, and gold as well. I was mesmerized as I stared at the little robotic elves as they loaded the sleigh, watched Santa in his rocker smoking his pipe and checking his list, and they even had a little dog running in circles for no apparent reason other than for the amusement of the viewers. I could have stared at that display for hours, but it was cold and my dad said we had to go, so we did."

"Taylor, those are beautiful memories. I knew you were an old softie deep down. You see, there is beauty all around us, but sometimes life grays them over."

The two continued their walk and finally stumbled upon the perfect Scotch pine. Once they agreed, Taylor submerged himself with the saw under the canopy of low hanging branches. Anyone who has ever performed this maneuver will attest to the fact that it can be a cussing good time. One could almost see Taylor's colorful lingo as it steamed from his mouth while he leaned down towards the ground in the bitter cold while struggling with the saw.

"Are you sure this is worth it?" he yelled.

When the deed was done and the bounty harvested, Taylor grabbed the base, Kaylee the tip, and the two marched their way to the gate to pay a ransom of forty-five dollars.

Once the tree was roped and secured in the trunk, Kaylee and Taylor walked back into the store, or converted shed as it actually was, to catch their breaths and warm up a bit under the guise of shopping for some holiday goodies.

Taylor said, "Man, it is more than nippy out. Have you ever been to California for Christmas?"

"I've never even been west of the Mississippi."

"Would you consider it? It's beautiful out there around that time of year. The temp is still in the upper seventies."

"Well, we just bought this tree. I wouldn't want it to go to waste. Besides, they said that there's a better than even chance that we might see a white Christmas this year."

"They always say that. They said that nearly every year when I was growing up, but I'll be damned if I ever saw one."

"Oh come on, there had to be at least one snowy Christmas."

"Not that I can recall, but then again if you lived at my house, nothing was rosy. Many occasions that should have been happy were over-shadowed by the numerous distressing events that took place under that roof. If alcohol was involved, and it usually was, Thanksgiving usually turned into a shouting match, birthdays weren't celebrated, and Christmas was always a strain. After times like that, one tends to recall only the negative."

Taylor continued, "I remember one time, Mom and Dad argued so much about whose in-laws' house to travel to on Christmas Eve, that dad took the tree out back and set fire to it. I guess he figured that if there was no tree, there would be no Christmas. He was right. That ended that Christmas."

"That's horrible."

"I suppose, but in later years, it became a cruel joke. You know, one of those episodes you look back upon and laugh about, but in reality you wish had never happened. Life there could be so bizarre on occasion that sometimes I used to wonder if many of those things actually happened at all, and yet I know they did."

"I'm sorry, Taylor. I didn't know you had it so rough."

"How would you? You just met me."

"I know, but you don't…"

114

"Don't look it?"

"Well…"

"Okay, so you don't want to spend Christmas in sunny California. How about the week before? You have some PTO coming your way, don't you?"

Kaylee was hesitant in answering because she realized she was walking into some uncharted territory with respect to her relationship with Taylor.

"I suppose I do. What are we actually talking about here? This is all so new," she said, followed by an uneasy chuckle.

"I don't know. I thought we could visit the town and stay at my place. I have to check in there anyway and make sure Jerry hasn't ripped off my gold albums and pawned them for gambling money. And to answer your question, yes, I do have more than one bedroom there. I have five of them to be exact."

"Well…"

"Then we could do some Christmas shopping out there…on Rodeo Drive."

"Oh, now you're talking!"

"Sure, shoes, shoes, shoes, as far as the eye can see. Good ones, too. Then there are jewelry stores, fancy perfumes, thongs…"

"Thongs?"

"Underwear. You know, lingerie."

"I know what they are! Leave my underwear out of it."

"Okay then, I'll be brief." Taylor followed that remark with a guffaw.

"Oh, you're awfully funny. Good Lord, could you see me in a thong?"

"Hmm," Taylor mused as he stared off into space to actually picture that image.

"Don't look at me! Sheesh, you perve!" she yelled, as she waved her mitten-covered hands in front of his face as if to distract him and erase that image from his mind.

A couple standing nearby snickered, and Kaylee was now embarrassed.

"Okay, forget I said anything. But they do have nice things there. How about it? It would broaden your horizons."

"Sounds interesting. I might. Let me think about it."

Kaylee knew from the first mention of the trip she would be interested in the venture. She had never been to L.A., and the chance to travel there with someone who actually knew the town was a plus. But she and Taylor were still an unknown. She had seen him at his worst and hoped his best would be better.

The following week, Kaylee gave a 'thumbs up' to the trip, and Taylor seemed thrilled. It was the first time since he moved back home that he seemed truly enthusiastic about anything. In fact, since Thanksgiving, his outlook on life seemed to change for the better. He actually put on a bit of weight during the last couple of weeks and was looking healthier and more robust. As far as L.A. went, I thought he was done with that town, at least that's what he said, but apparently a visit would be bearable if he had someone to share his time with.

During the couple of weeks leading up to their trip, Taylor and the school assembly band traveled to the junior high schools and put on the 'band drive' concert. It went quite well, to be honest, and the talk around school was that the stigma of being a band geek was going by the wayside. The students were actually thinking that Taylor was on to something pretty 'rad.'

Being satisfied with their efforts of the last few weeks, Taylor and Kaylee packed for a week-long get-away beginning Saturday the eighteenth, and jetted off to LAX. Following an uneventful trip across the country, Kaylee became aware of just how big Taylor was in that town after they touched down.

First of all, she had never considered how the two of them would get from the airport to Taylor's mansion. She just assumed that they'd rent a car. Taylor rented a car alright, but it actually was a limousine. That would impress most people to be sure, but in that town, that mode of transportation isn't a rarity. "You can't sling a dead cat in this town without hitting a limo," Taylor once said. Kaylee was mostly impressed by the fact that the driver and Taylor were on a first-name basis.

To add to the unusual atmosphere of it all, when walking towards the baggage carrousel, a few people approached Taylor and asked him for his autograph. Taylor obliged, and the autograph hounds left satisfied.

Kaylee asked, "How in the world does anyone recognize you with your new haircut and all?"

"Ah, I'm not just another pretty face," he replied with a wry grin.

"God knows."

"What?"

"Nothing."

Taylor stared at Kaylee as they walked over to an open space near the conveyor, but she did her best to look straight ahead and hide her smirk. It was a struggle she was losing with each step. Taylor threw his arm around her shoulder and gave her a hug.

"You're a clown, you know that?"

The two gathered their bags up and made their way to the pickup lane. The stretch limo was waiting for them, and while the driver loaded their gear, Taylor held the door for Kaylee.

The limo's interior was dim, and smelled of new leather and Double Mint gum. "Oh my, this is nice. I don't think I've ever been in a limo before, except when my grandmother passed away when I was eleven. That was a long time ago."

"Where to, Mr. Ross?" asked Larry Adams, the driver.

"Home, Lar."

"No town surfing?"

"Not today. We'll probably check things out tomorrow."

"Well, you picked a great time to visit. The town's in for a fine stretch of weather. The temp is supposed to get up to seventy-five in the day, and won't dip below fifty overnight for a low."

"That's excellent, Lar. Beautiful Christmas weather!" he bellowed.

Taylor hit the button, raising the glass partition between the driver's seat and the passenger compartment. He turned to Kaylee and said, "He treats me like gold because I'm a generous tipper."

"I see. I guess money speaks volumes out here."

"It's the universal language."

It was just past four in the afternoon as the limo wound its way past Santa Monica, through Brentwood, then made the proverbial cut-off at Encino. Nearly forty-five minutes after they left the airport, they pulled into Taylor's Rockwood estate. Larry pulled the car around the crescent-shaped driveway and stopped in front of the entrance.

As the two stepped out of the back seat, Taylor proclaimed, "Well, welcome to California. What do you think?"

Kaylee looked around at the estate with its beautifully landscaped grounds, then glanced towards the mountainous horizon as she attempted to take in all of the atmosphere of this new world that she had only heard of and seen on television. To say it was a surreal experience for her would be an understatement.

"Oh my, it's so warm out here. It feels like early summer," she said as she threw her arms out and did a complete spin. Kaylee breathed in the warm, dry air and followed it up with an "Mmm," sound.

"See, if you moved out here, this could be an everyday experience," Taylor said.

"I know, but I'd miss working with the kids. Plus, as nice as this is, a Christmas without cold temperatures just doesn't seem like Christmas."

"I see. I'll tell you what, let's head inside and see what kind of mess I left back in September. To be honest, I'm not sure what we'll find. I wasn't actually in the best frame of mind when I left here."

"Is that why you left?"

Taylor didn't answer.

When they walked up to the front door, Taylor raised his hand to the security keypad, then hesitated. He was trying to remember the password. "It's been a while," he said, followed by a small chuckle. After another few seconds, he cautiously tapped in a code, received the green light, then opened the door allowing the three of them to enter. Once again, Kaylee was filled with a sense of awe. She admired the cathedral ceiling in the entranceway, then gazed out into the main room.

"This is beautiful," she stated. "Oh my, Taylor, this is a palace."

Taylor was busy stuffing Larry's hands with cash. To Kaylee he said, "Oh, thank you. It's home, at least it was." Turning to Larry he said, "Two of the best T-bones you can find, and maybe a couple of baking potatoes. Lar, you know you're certainly welcome to…"

"Oh no, no. I'm not going to get in the way. Three's a crowd, don't you know."

"Oh Lar, it's nothing like that. We're just friends."

"Uh huh. All of the way from Ohio, and staying a week with the great meat-master? She doesn't stand a chance."

"If you want to keep that tip, you'll keep your mouth shut and bring that stuff back here as soon as possible. Step on it."

"Yes sir."

Getting back to the previous conversation, he said, "Well, thank you, Kay. I'm actually thinking of selling it though."

"Selling it? Why?"

"Well, in living here, I isolated myself. I cut myself off from the rest of the world. That might have served its purpose in its day, but I've been thinking lately that I might be ready to rejoin the living."

The two began a tour of the house. Taylor took her down one of the hallways towards the den. Hanging along the way were a few concert photos from the day, as well as Taylor's copies of Vulture's gold records. He used to refer to this hallway as his hall of fame.

"Oh my God, look at the sideburns!" Kaylee did her best to stifle her laugh.

"Yeah, that's an early one. You have to remember it was still around the time of Woodstock and the like. It was one hell of a time to be around."

"Did you ever get your picture on the cover of the Rolling Stone, as the old song used to say?"

"Cover? I wasn't on the cover, but there were so many stories and interviews of us inside over the years. Many, many photographs as well. There was the infamous black cover Rolling Stone put out with just our logo on the front. Oh, here it is, right here. Check it out."

"Wow, that is you! I'll be darned, a white, wicked-looking 'V' on a black background. Pretty." The two took another few steps and came to Vulture's awards.

"This is impressive," she said as she glanced at the first, then to a half dozen more record plaques. "I hate to plead ignorance, but exactly what constitutes a gold record?"

"Well, it depends who you're talking to. In the U.S., the RIAA, or Recording Industry Association of America, designates that 500,000 copies have to be shipped or sold for that piece to qualify as a gold album, and time generally isn't a factor. A platinum album is one million in sales."

"Oh, I see. My, how impressive," she commented as she walked down Taylor's hall of fame and read off the titles. "*Light of the Moon.*"

"Yep, our inaugural album and it went platinum X, twenty-X to date. That doesn't happen too often. It was a bit of a themed album, kind of like Sergeant Pepper's, and that's rare for an initial effort. It was like, you know, the birth of an ideal with the vulture emerging under the light of the moon as opposed to a phoenix rising from the sun. It was a bit goth before Ozzie and the like. The whole thing was John's idea. The guy was a musical genius in his day, I'll give him that. Anyway, because of that little innovation, I guess you could say that *Light of the Moon* was the horse we rode in on. We used to joke that we started at the top, and worked our way to the bottom. Well, we didn't really, but it was our best seller having sold over twenty million copies to date. That's as many cuts as The Beatles' White Album, or Pink Floyd's *Dark Side of the Moon* sold, just to give you some perspective. Speaking of which, I'll say to my dying day that *Light of the Moon* was a driving influence for Pink Floyd's *Dark Side* album. Oh sure, our music was a bit harder and more basic than theirs, but the concept was there. But then again, in the music business, everyone begs, borrows, and steals from everyone else. It's just the way it is."

"It was that good, huh?"

"It was better than good," he said with nothing but sincerity in his eyes. "We were so hungry and so full of creativity; everything just jelled. We were so advanced despite our lack of experience. During the 1969 Grammy Awards, we were in line for the album of the year, but we were beaten out by that dumb-ass Glen Campbell for *By The Time I Get To Phoenix*. I guess they felt we hadn't paid our dues yet. We were supposed to be the dumb-asses up there on stage."

Kaylee laughed because she knew Taylor didn't realize what he just said.

"We finished the album up with a heavy metal rendition of *By the Light of the Silvery Moon*. Now, I would have bet that it was impossible to make that song rock, but John put his own little twist to it, and it worked. He had a twisted mind. I miss his creativity."

*"Pickin' on Sunset & Vine."*

"That was a favorite. It was our only live album, and it was us hitting our stride early. That's when we really built our fan base. We recorded it at the Hollywood Palladium during the Pop Expo '69. Rolling Stone described that album as our soul laid bare. They were right."

"Featuring their number one song, *Boom Daddy, Boom*."

"Do you remember that one? It's one of the songs that put us on the map. Remember how that one went?"

"Didn't it go something like…You're going to scream and shout, boom daddy, boom, when I'm goin' in and out…"

"Yeah, and then everybody in the audience would yell, "Boom daddy, boom!" Yeah, that was our one big audience participation song. We had to do it at nearly every concert after that. We wrote it in about an hour."

"Why am I not surprised? You guys were a bunch of pervs."

"What? That song was referring to going in and out of the room. Why, what did you think it meant?"

"Yeah right." Kaylee wasn't easily fooled. "Real high-brow music."

"It was a gimmick, and let's face it, sex sells, even implied sex. Choir boys we weren't."

Taking one step to the left, he continued, "Next to that is our album *Live From Carrion*, speaking of gimmicks. It was a good follow-up though. Those two albums were like *Pickin'* one and two. They could have been a double album because they were so much alike, and we contemplated that, but we decided to give them a twist. We went live with one, and did the other in a studio. Ironically, *Pickin'* was live while *Live* wasn't."

"With songs like *Mild to Late Seven*, go figure."

"We used some sound effects ala The Beatles to provide some canned crowd sounds to give the illusion that it was recorded live, but it was so synthesized that everyone knew it wasn't. It was like a parody of a concert. That's what made it so unique. Through it all though, it worked out because more albums meant more money."

"So you were human after all."

"Yep, we were sell-outs, and all the while acting as if we were dedicated to our craft. Actually, we were on both accounts. We thought we were on a roll then, but all good things must come to an end, as they say."

"*Summer Lucky?*"

"Yes, as I was saying. *Summer Lucky* was a bust. I think John was trying to give a nod to the Beach Boys' album *Pet Sounds*. He used to hang with the Wilson brothers a bit. Some saw it as a sell-out, you know, following a style rather than setting the trend. The album didn't work, in my opinion, but we were popular enough to go gold with it. Some people will buy anything, I suppose. It was one of John's last albums with us, at least as a leader and full time member."

"Okay, then we have *Scavengin' For a Livin,'* and *Top of the Heap.*"

"Those were the two I put together. With John AWOL for the most part, I managed to infuse some popularity back into the group, and we had a couple of number one cuts off each album including *Mistress in a Silver Spoon*. That was a shot at John's current lifestyle. I wasn't real happy with him at that point. Even though taking over the group was a blessing in disguise for me, I thought it was a pain in the ass at the time. I thought John was a pain in the ass. As a result, the last cut on *Top of the Heap* was titled *One Man Banned.*"

They moved on. "Finally we have *Fly-By-Night Operation.*"

"Yeah, that was our wrap up, our swan song, to coin a phrase," Taylor said with a downcast voice. "Even as the cover suggests, *Fly By Night* was almost like the anti-*Light of the Moon*. We really weren't hitting it off at that point, as a group or individuals, if you know what I mean. Okay, were at each other's throats. But through it all, we managed to show up and finish the album, even if it was on separate days and on separate tracks. It's a shame too because that album might have been one of our finest, musically speaking. The theme of the album brought us full circle as a group. Get it, *Light of the Moon*, to *Fly-By-Night Operation?*"

"I see. Well I'm impressed, I have to say."

"Thank you. In total, we sold more than seventy-five million covers and counting. Not bad for a group that put out only seven main albums. We have a few 'best of' albums as well as compilations out there as well, but these original seven were our mainstay. That seventy-five million units is as many as Van Halen sold during their heyday, or KISS for that matter. In fact, a lot of people thought of us as a forerunner of KISS, without the costumes, make-up, and all. We didn't need gimmicks. We weren't a circus show. We were who we were. We went where the music took us."

"Do you miss those guys any, your old band mates?"

"Eh, occasionally but not really. I mean, we had our run. It was time to move on, not to mention that I probably drove them away. I tend to do that to people. If they don't drive me away first, I end up chasing them away." After a pause, he cleared his mind and continued, "Speaking of moving on, there's plenty of house left to see."

Taylor walked Kaylee around the house, and she experienced mixed feelings inside. You see, Taylor came across as a somewhat unkempt individual when she first met him, yet his home, while sparsely furnished, was so orderly and tastefully decorated.

"Now, out here is the deck," he said as he unlatched, then opened the sliding glass door. It took a couple of tugs as it had been a few months since that door had been opened.

"I spent many a morning and night out here. It was usually too hot during the day, except for this time of year." As he looked around, Taylor commented, "Man, this place needs a good sweeping. I'll get the broom and give it quick dusting. Larry is bringing a couple of steaks back to the house for us and I thought we'd cook out. It's a beautiful evening for it. I didn't think you wanted to go out to eat, having flown all day."

Taylor began sweeping, and Kaylee looked around to see what she could do to tidy up the place. She saw the bucket Taylor used to extinguish his joints. Taylor noticed. He went over to move it out of the way.

"That damn Jerry. He must have been partying and, you know, things like that."

"Uh huh."

Kaylee pulled the cover off the grill and began checking it out. She pronounced it worthy, and the propane tank was still nearly full.

Larry showed back up and Taylor met him in the kitchen.

"Taylor, I did better than T-bones. Look, filet mignons. Huh?"

"Damn Sam, Lar, those things are so thick that they'll never get done. Why didn't you…"

"Boys, don't worry. I'll just butterfly them and all will be fine. Thanks Larry."

"Yes ma'am. Take care, you two. And Taylor, if you need anything, give me a call. I'm open much of the week, and I'm a little short, you know."

"That's okay. We'll probably drive the A.M. into town all week; that is, if it starts. I put a trickle charger on it before I left. We will need a ride to the airport next Friday morning though. Keep six AM open to LAX."

"Will do."

Kaylee laid out the package on the counter and looked around for a knife suitable for the operation. She took a step and heard something crunch under her feet. She bent down and picked up a small shard of glass.

"Oh my, this will ruin your floor if someone grinds it into the laminate."

"The floor is genuine wood, actually. Sorry about that. I must have dropped a glass while doing the dishes a while ago. It's been so long."

Kaylee searched for more, and found a few scattered chips, then continued her preparation.

Dinner went well. In fact, Taylor commented that it must have been the finest meal ever prepared at this house. "It almost makes this place seem like a home."

"Why, because Larry did indeed buy the finest steaks?"

"Maybe." Then, after a pause he said, "Maybe it was the company."

The following day was spent recovering from the jet lag. Taylor planned to take Kaylee to Capitol Records on Monday and show her a bit of the industry. As his landline had been disconnected some time ago, he picked up his cell phone and called someone in charge at Capitol, to set up a tour for Monday around midday.

The next day, they cruised to downtown Los Angeles and shopped around for a parking place for ten minutes. Shortly after they checked in, a man named Don Cooke came down and welcomed the two.

"Taylor, wow, it's been a long time-too long. How have you been, my man?"

"I'm doing pretty damn good," he said, rather matter-of-factly. "You're still here? Man, that's wild."

"Yes sir. Do you have a hankering to get back in the biz? A lot of groups would like to have you as a featured player. You can still burn it up, can't you?"

"I can still handle it, but I have other obligations right now. Thanks for the invite, though."

Taylor and Kaylee were escorted to Studio C, Taylor's favorite, and upon entering, he was impressed by the visual advancements alone that had been made to the studio. One thing that hadn't changed was the clash of personalities that Taylor used to experience with the sound crews. For whatever reason, he rarely saw eye-to-eye with those people. Perhaps it was because he always referred to those people as 'those people.'

"Oh yeah, everything's digital now. We operate Studer eight-twenty-sevens, Ampex ATR one zero two, dash one zero fours, Apogee two-TK converters…"

"Whoa, all of that stuff's over my head."

"Yep, it's not like the old RCA reel-to-reel stuff you guys used back in the old days."

"Well, all of our material sounded pretty damn good. Still does."

129

"What, on your eight track player?" The others in the booth laughed.

"We have material out on digital media now that sounds just as good as anything you guys can produce today."

"That's because we've digitally remastered all of your old material. We cleaned all of the background hiss out of the tapes. A lot of changes have occurred, and not just cosmetic ones." He held up something that looked like a cross between an old three-and-a-half inch computer floppy, and a compact flash memory card. "That's all your career is today, my man; a three inch square piece of plastic."

One of the staff members asked Taylor if he'd like to watch one of their premier bands, D-Member, do a take on their first disc. Taylor agreed. "This will give you some idea of what we went through for those fifteen-plus years," he told Kaylee.

When they begin to play, Taylor winced. To say the least, their style of playing was nothing like Vulture. In fact, I doubt you could even classify D-Member's genre as rock and roll. I'm not sure what style it is to this day, perhaps some sort of urban-rock-hip-hop music, but I do know that it wasn't to Taylor's liking.

Kaylee noticed Taylor's irritation. D's sound was just too harsh, even for him. Time had taken its toll on Taylor's ears as well, and they just weren't able to withstand the racket like they could when he was younger. After a minute of enduring this noise, Kaylee quietly asked, "Do you want to go?"

"Let's hit it."

Taylor bid the folks in the booth a silent goodbye, then shut the door quietly behind them.

As they walked down the hall towards the elevator, Kaylee noticed that Taylor seemed a bit irritated. "My God, that crap can't be what sells today."

"Oh yes, the students listen to music like that all of the time in the hallways at Hamilton."

"Don't flatter it by calling it music. That crap only masquerades as music."

"That, coming from a man who's supposed to lead the band playing marches next fall."

"That's different. A marching band, by definition, is a collection of people uniting for the purpose of producing inspiring music through the collaboration of the woodwind, percussion, and brass sections."

"You've been looking up too many websites."

"Where was the melody in that crap-rock-stuff those guys were playing? Did you hear it? Did you feel it? Did you see it? There was no conviction in their eyes. There was no connection to their soul. It was all mechanical, computer-generated crap, and please don't call chanting singing. I heard absolutely nothing creative from those musicians, if that's what you want to call them."

"You're showing your age, my dear."

"I'm relaying my acquired musical knowledge."

The two exited the building on to Vine, and Taylor indecisively looked around as if searching out the couple's next destination. He walked over to a bench and sat down until he could come to a decision.

"You know, back in my day, we were dedicated to our music. We weren't hell-bent on being famous or earning a huge buck."

"Oh no? What about the two albums instead of one?"

"That was a business decision not of our making. Creatively, we went where the music took us, and society told music where they wanted to go. Our path was dictated to us by our spirit, therefore by the will of the people."

"The times change, and so does the music."

"You know," he continued, "I met Neil Young a few times. You've heard of him. At first, I thought his singing was dreadful. But the more I listened to it, the more I realized that it was so consistently bad, to my ears, that it was actually good," he stated as he looked up at her. "It was perfect."

"See, maybe D-Member's sound will grow on you."

"Well, let me finish. Neil was way out there, musically I mean, but talk about dedication," he said with a shake of the head. "The man was possessed by his music. He basically said that it owned him, not the other way around. We as a group, or individuals for that matter, never got to that stage in our music making. Well, maybe John did early on, but in my opinion, those people up there in Studio C were forcing the issue. They were in it for a buck, in my opinion. You can't do that with music and expect to become successful."

"Success is in the eye of the beholder."

"Are you defending them?"

"No, but I'm closer to their age than you are. I understand that this might be their path in life. There is no right road to take, and the road to success is paved much differently than in your day. It just depends on what kind of ride you prefer."

Taylor looked at her for a moment, sighed, then said, "Maybe you're right. Maybe I am feeling my age. Maybe life has passed me by."

"Taylor, you were a success because you earned what you sought. But earning that same respect today is a whole different ballgame; not better or worse, just different."

"Different is right. You know, when disco music came into being during the mid to late 1970s, that's when the true rock era imploded, in my opinion. Everything musically was built on a concept of glitz rather than conveying a message of societal importance. In the early days, rock music stood for controlled rebellion; you know, do your own thing, but let's do it together. Later, music expanded upon that theme and demanded that the people rise up and rebel against the values society held tried and true. 'Be who you were meant to be rather than taking the easy way out and decaying spiritually in the cubby hole society puts you in based on your gender, race, or ethnicity,' they said."

"So, I assume that was the end of your era, musically speaking. Where have you been since then?"

"I'm not sure. For the most part, I've been right here," he said while pointing to his chest, his inner soul. "Searching, I suppose."

"And did you find what you were looking for?"

Taylor looked Kaylee in the eyes. "I think so." He stood up and took her hand. "Let's go."

"Where to?"

"I don't know. Some place nicer than this."

"How about some of that great shopping you promised me on Rodeo Drive?"

"To the round-up it is."

The two drove over to the infamous avenue of expensive treats. From Gucci to Gianfranco Ferre, from Luis Vuitton to Hermes, Kaylee just stared in awe as they drove past stores she once only dreamed of patronizing.

"Look at that, they have shrubbery growing on the roof of that store." They did indeed, but that would be mildest of sights she would see on this afternoon. She was also impressed that the street light standards were dressed up for the holidays to resemble gift boxes around the bases, and clear packages complete with bows for lamp shades. Only on Rodeo.

After driving around the block twice, they finally found a parking spot.

"Where do you want to begin?"

Kaylee was like a kid in a candy store at this point. "I-I don't know. I mean, it's all so-"

"Yes, it can be a bit overwhelming. I'll tell you what," Taylor said with a laugh, "how about if we just window shop down this side of the street, then the other. If you see anything you're interested in, make a note of it and we can come back to it."

It was agreed, and the two began their hike, but they didn't make it past the second block before Kaylee ducked into one of the businesses to browse. They entered Ralph Lauren to peruse the merchandise for a while, then moved on. Kaylee eventually spotted

Prada, known worldwide for their fine footwear. She actually ran towards the establishment yelling, "You promised me shoes, shoes, and more shoes. This is where I want to shop!" And so they did.

Kaylee, trying not to go overboard, purchased two pairs of shoes from that establishment, then they once again moved on. They walked and talked, Kaylee sometimes carrying the bag, while Taylor toted it the majority of the time. They passed by a golden reflective window in one of the shops, and Taylor stopped. He then began to laugh. Kaylee backed up to join him and see what was so funny.

"Look at that, Taylor said. "We look like a couple, a real couple." Kaylee had to laugh too because the sight of the pair, Kaylee with her purse in hand, and Taylor toting a bag of items Kaylee purchased, mirrored that of a very married couple.

"Oh my, let's go." The two resumed their hike.

Walking past one of the decorated light standards put Taylor in mind of a song Vulture recorded. "You know," Taylor began, "I think I wrote only one Christmas song."

"*Only* one? I'd be impressed at just one."

"Yep. It was called *It's not Christmas if Your Car's on Fire*."

"Oh, that's horrible."

"I thought so too, but the thinking back then was, if you couldn't eat it or screw it, you might as well burn it. You have to remember, it was the time of societal heat; you know, Jimi Hendrix's song *Fire*, James Taylor's ballad *Fire and Rain*, and Stokely Carmichael's 'burn baby, burn' speech. But that was back in the old days. The song fit in with the turbulent times, I suppose. You'd be surprised how many people actually liked it. They still play it

135

occasionally as a novelty holiday classic. I guess there's no accounting for taste."

They turned and began walking up the incline at the fork in the road when Kaylee stopped and began staring at some jewelry in the window of one of the stores. The prices were outrageous of course, and while she thought most of the items were just too gaudy for her taste, she did see a ring, presumably an engagement ring, that impressed her greatly.

"Look at that. Oh, that is beautiful. If I ever get married, that's the kind of ring I would like."

"Ten thousand bucks? I hope you land some rich dude."

"I might just do…" she stopped. Kaylee realized that she was dreaming. "You know what; I'm way out of my league here." She gave an uneasy laugh.

"Oh, I wouldn't say that. You'd be like that babe we sang about in our song *One Classy Broad*. We sang, "She was a woman of class, when sporting a handful of glass…" I won't repeat the rest of the phrase. You can guess."

"I can imagine. Do you think I'm one classy broad?"

Trying to sound like actor Jackie Gleason playing Ralph Kramden on *The Honeymooners* television show, he threw his arm around her and said, "Baby, you're the greatest."

Kaylee laughed. "You are such a nut. I'll tell you what–how about if we get a bite to eat, then head back to the house."

"That's a plan."

The two finished out their evening at one of the finer restaurants, then retired to Rockwood. They spent the remainder of the week taking in the sights of that magnificent town. On Tuesday, they traveled to Hollywood Boulevard and viewed the Walk of Fame, Grauman's Chinese Theater, and went through The Hollywood History Museum. The following day they took in a tour at Paramount Studios, then visited some of the residents at a couple of the Hollywood cemeteries. On Thursday, they walked around the Griffith Park Observatory. "We did up the town," Taylor said.

On their final day, Friday, Taylor and Kaylee pretty much stuck around Rockwood and cleaned the place up. Taylor packed some of his clothes that he planned to take to Ohio. Taylor told Kaylee to plan on a late dinner, as he would like to take her on a hike through the canyon in the late afternoon. The temperature hit seventy-two that day, so the hike sounded ideal.

Kaylee spent much of her time that afternoon cleaning out the refrigerator. Taylor probably wouldn't need anything in there for the foreseeable future. He wasn't even sure when he would get back there.

While spiffing the place up, Kaylee came across a potted, orange-sized cactus in the windowsill in Taylor's kitchen. Taylor noticed her looking the plant over as it had just begun to sprout a pea-sized magenta-colored flower.

"There's a story behind that little plant," he said as he walked over towards the window. "One day right after I moved into this place, I was walking around the perimeter and found this little cactus bulldozed over in the corner of the lot. It was the size of a golf ball back then. I felt sorry for it, so I picked it up gingerly. Man, was it spiney. It took some patience, but I managed to get it into a pot, and after some time, a little love, and a spot of water, it took root. That was a feat unto itself because it had very little root base to begin with, but I guess it liked me. I've changed its pot several times when it outgrew the old one, and it's always a painful experience, but I survived. As the years went by, I took care of it, gave it a little fertilizer, and now it has become productive and even sprouted an offspring. I separated it and potted it, and now it's the size of the original mother plant. Just look at them now. See what a little love can do?"

Kaylee said, "Yeah, and a lot of fertilizer."

After they finished the task at hand and took one last look around, Taylor told Kaylee that he'd made up his mind and that he might as well put the place up for sale.

"Why, Taylor? This is a beautiful place."

"I think I'm content staying where I currently am. This place has served its purpose, and I think I've moved on."

Taylor left to finish up his packing. Kaylee just stared at the cactus.

Around four o'clock, Taylor figured they had everything squared away. "How about taking in some of the canyon to blow off some steam, then we can catch a dinner back here?"

"That will work. As nice as this place is, there's a lot of cleaning involved."

The two began their slow descent into the canyon. "Don't worry about rattlers. They're not much for the cooler weather."

"Oh, that's wonderful. Now you tell me."

Kaylee and Taylor traveled the well-worn path he used to know all too well. He probably could have navigated it blindfolded. Taylor had nearly memorized every rut and rock outcropping along each inch of the trail. On this day, he noticed that very little had changed. It rarely did in this area.

The seasons did change, however, even in sunny California. The smell of drying hillside brush, mixed with flowering plants whose productive days were numbered, gave off a fragrance that Taylor found all too familiar. He said that it wasn't completely different from what he experienced during the fall season back when he grew up in Ohio, but he definitely could tell the two apart. Still, the aromas of fall, no matter what part of the country they originated from, tended to cast a veil of depression over him, Taylor once said. That was natural, for the end of a season of growth can only be followed by a period of lifelessness. Such is life.

For years, Taylor spent many a day hiking this same path 'hoping to find himself,' as he put it. So today, in order to silence the ghosts of yesteryear, he wanted to take one final expedition to the land that never was. You see, he used to deal with his inner pain, the spiritual anguish that had become his constant companion over the years, by journeying to this destination and imagining that he was in another world, another dimension, if you will. I suppose it soothed him for a brief period of time. It was either that, or the weed he had just smoked had done its thing. Either way, we all seek our own channels of escape throughout life. For that stage of his life, this had been Taylor's.

They finally arrived at a small body of water that was pond-like in size. It was the Franklin Canyon Reservoir. This area has been used during the filming of several television shows and movies. Taylor related to this area as Myer's Lake, made famous when Opie skipped the rock across the water during the opening of *The Andy*

*Griffith Show* filmed back in the early 1960s. In reality, this pool is a water reservoir for the city of Los Angeles and surrounding area. There is a hiking path around it, and Taylor directed the way.

He and Kaylee hiked around the rim for five minutes until they came upon a bench somewhere midway around the pond.

"Let's light here for a while."

The two took a seat, and neither one said a word for nearly ten minutes. Taylor would look out across the water for some time, then glance down while dismantling a slender twig. Kaylee could tell that Taylor was deep within himself, and she presumed that this area meant more to him than just a stop-off point during a hike. She let him be.

Finally, Taylor spoke up. "You know, I used to think this was the greatest place in the world; Myer's Lake. It was on the edge of Mayberry, USA. From here, there had to be another dimension close by where I could just step through and enter the town that was perfect. It seemed that every day in Mayberry was summer, and there was always time to fish, enjoy friends, and have picnics. People there could actually live and be who they were meant to be without worrying about any unfavorable judgment. Oh, Mayberry had its problems, but nothing the sheriff couldn't handle. The deputy was harmless and the jail rarely used. You lived next to peaceful neighbors, you worked hard, you attended church each Sunday, you enjoyed each other's company, and at the end of the day, you could sit out on the front porch and just take it all in. Let's face it, Mayberry was equipped with everything an individual needed to live a harmonious life. It was western civilization's answer to Shangri-La, or so I used to think."

Kaylee just stared at Taylor and was beginning to recognize that he was much deeper than even she realized.

"It was all so close, you know, and I dreamed that someday I would find that portal and make it to the other side." Taylor then barked a small, sarcastic laugh. "Shows how naïve, and frankly, messed-up I was. I'll bet I wasted a large portion of my life here dreaming of the impossible."

"Taylor, it seems that everything I see out here I find to be beautiful, yet you see just the opposite. Am I missing something?"

"Yes. You look with your eyes. I see with my soul. You just had to be here, I guess. You see, I used my house here as a buffer from the real world, and I used this spot as an escape from my life. But just this week, I came to the realization that my problems, and the pain I experienced in the world as I saw it, emanated from within. I spent all of my time blaming my parents, my band mates, and the world in general. The sins of the father have visited the son, I thought."

"Taylor, you coped the best way you knew how. You journeyed here to this pond and managed to make it all of the way to Mayberry, at least in spirit. That's a long way from the trials and tribulations of everyday life. That little town provided shelter for your soul until you were able to move on. That's a gift, and it served itself well. Let's face it, none of us come with a Life 101 manual."

"Well, I finally figured out that there's one thing I couldn't escape: My own soul. It didn't matter if I retreated from the world through a physical means, or if I withdrew mentally or spiritually like I've been doing for most of my life. One's only option is to look back on their life's circumstances and realize that things just are, and the only alternative is to deal with it to the best of our ability. Better on this side of the turf as opposed to the opposite, huh?"

"I agree. It sounds like you've learned quite a lot since moving from the area. I guess it's all about what you do from here on out that really counts."

"I guess it's the first time I've seen this place in a sober light."

"Good for you, Taylor. Look at it this way; everything you've done thus far has brought you to this moment and place in your life. This is a giant turning point for you. There's still plenty of time for you make up for all of life's lost opportunities. I'm glad that you stuck around. The world, and the band, would be far worse off without you."

"Ah yes, the band. I almost forgot about that situation. What are we going to do about that?"

"We'll just keep on punching away until we see daylight. We'll get there, Taylor."

Taylor let out a large sigh. "I hope so. The task seems so daunting. I can usually set a goal, then achieve it. That's the way I've always lived my life. But now…"

"Tay, one step at a time."

"One day at a time. Where have I heard that before? Don't answer that."

After another minute of silence, Kaylee spoke up. "Oh, it's beginning to get a bit chilly out here."

"That it is. It's time for us to head back up to the house. If we stay out too long, we might meet the coyotes face to face. When it gets cool out, they like to roam just after sundown."

"Goodness, then let's make a break for it."

142

"We have time. I've never seen a coyote out here, I've only heard them."

"Much like your fears?"

Taylor just looked at Kaylee and marveled at her wisdom. The two turned to made their way up the bank with Kaylee leading. I think she took the coyote thing seriously. Anyway, she stopped and noticed that Taylor was still on the water's edge. He just stared at the pond and surrounding terrain for a spell. It was as if he wanted last look at his unholy refuge, kiss it good-bye, then move on. He picked up a rock as if he was going to skip it across the water as he had done many times before, but decided to do otherwise and joined Kaylee on their journey back to the house.

They made it back with little more than an occasional scratch, ate dinner, then cleaned up. It was dark by now, and the two decided it would be for the best if they turned in early so they could get a sunrise start back home. Neither of them was too keen on leaving. Taylor had made peace with his house and surrounding grounds, and within his soul to be honest, and Kaylee had taken a shine to the warm weather. But they both knew it was time to move on. They had things waiting on them back at home.

To complicate matters, snow was predicted in Cincinnati for their Christmas Eve arrival. That could mean in-air delays, or highway troubles once they arrived, and that is if they were able to land. In their favor, the snow wasn't predicted to start until midday, so it was going to be close.

Taylor turned in, Kaylee checked on him, then made one last tour around the house to make sure everything that was going back home with them was packed. As she scanned the area, Taylor's cactus plant caught her eye as it was sitting all alone on the windowsill. She walked over to it. After a period of time, she made a decision. She reached over to a pile of junk that had been tagged as waste, took an empty box from the mess, then gently packed Taylor's cactus plant inside, along with some newspaper for filler. She set the sealed box next to their luggage, then turned off the light.

Morning came all too soon for the two. Both stumbled through their morning routines, then pronounced themselves as ready as they were going to be. Kaylee sensed that Taylor was a bit out of sorts, now that he was leaving his home, and leaving it a different person than he arrived. She allowed him his space as he first just stared around the vestibule, then she watched as he wandered around the front room a bit. What was going through his mind she didn't know, but she felt that it was important for him to depart the premises under his own terms.

The conditions would be dictated for him, however, as Larry pulled up in the limo and its honking horn echoed across the canyon. There was no other sound in the house, and Taylor finally broke the silence.

"Well, all ready?"

"I was going to ask you the same thing."

He took one last look around. "Yes, yes I'm ready. It's time to go."

They made it to the airport in time for their eight-thirty flight, and were nearing Cincinnati as the four o'clock hour rolled around.

"As we approach Greater Cincinnati Airport, ladies and gentlemen, the temperature is twenty-eight degrees, and they are receiving snow at the moment. We should experience no problem with the landing, but reports tell us that the weather will worsen as evening falls. Please be careful on your drive home. Thank you for flying with us and enjoy your stay."

Taylor continued to stare out the window, and he wasn't encouraged that he wasn't able to see ground until the aircraft was on its final approach. At that point, all he saw was a blanket of white coating the ground, and he was able to make out only a few of the support buildings at the airport. The long-promised Christmas Eve snow hadn't made liars out of the weather forecasters this time.

"Oh Lord, how are we going to get out of this mess?" he asked.

"Slow but sure. We'll take it a step at a time." Taylor glanced Kaylee's way.

They did just that. Step one was the departure from the aircraft, step two was to collect their luggage, and finally step three had them locate their vehicle and make a break for it.

They made it to step three, but it seemed as if no one else wanted to cooperate. A trip that ordinarily takes an hour or so turned into a two-and-a-half fiasco. They had to make their way around cars that had spun into the ditch line, and a few that had stalled out in the middle of the freeway.

Just before eight o'clock, they pulled into Kaylee's driveway. By now, there was nearly six inches of the white stuff piled up on the ground.

As they ran towards the house with what luggage they could carry, Kaylee shouted, "Well, you can no longer say that you've never seen a white Christmas!"

"Shut up and open the door!"

She did, and Taylor made one last trip out to the car to fetch Kaylee's remaining luggage. When she began putting some of her things away, Taylor said, "Well, I guess you have quite a lot to do, laundry and all, so I'll head on out."

"You'll do nothing of the sort! Taylor Ross, you sit down and let me fix you something to eat. A couple of bags of Oreos on the plane isn't a fit meal for either of us."

Taylor did as he was told.

In a moment of playfulness, she shouted from the kitchen, "Hey, I still have some old turkey left over from Thanksgiving. How about a slippery turkey sandwich?"

"Very funny."

While she was throwing something simple together, Taylor went into the kitchen and grabbed a pitcher of water for the Christmas tree.

He crawled under the tree, moved the skirt and proclaimed, "Wow, is this thing ever dry."

"Brenda said that she was going to stop by and water it mid-week. How are the needles?"

"Actually, they feel okay," he said after raking his hand down one of the branches.

Having completed his task, Taylor laid for a moment, and just inhaled. The scent of pine filled his nostrils. The last time he had experienced such aromatic pleasure was when he was just a child playing with his trucks under the tree. He crawled out, switched the lights on, then stood in front of it for a spell to admire it. It had been quite a while since he had taken the time to enjoy a real Christmas tree in all its splendor. He then looked around and spotted Kaylee's fireplace.

"Hey, does this thing work, the fireplace I mean?"

"Sure. There's a pile of firewood out on the back porch."

"Wood?"

"Yes wood. Some fireplaces still burn the old-fashioned stuff, you know? They sell so many of them, you'd think they grew on trees!"

"Okay, okay. I was used to throwing a switch out at Rockwood and having it come on."

"The wood ought to be dry. It's covered. Check it, then make sure the damper is open on the chimney."

Taylor successfully started a fire, and the two ate dinner. Afterwards, they cooperated in clearing the table, then settled down to talk about their trip a bit. After a while, Taylor got up and made another trip out back for some additional firewood. Kaylee retreated to the kitchen.

"Wow, it's still coming down out here. You ought to see it!" he shouted from the porch.

"I saw it from the front. It's beautiful."

Taylor returned and stoked up the fire, and Kaylee entered the room with two drinks in her hands. She turned off the light switch with her elbow leaving the glow of the fireplace and the lights on the Christmas tree to illuminate the room.

"Isn't it beautiful?"

"Yes, I have to admit that I can't remember seeing a more beautiful holiday sight in recent memory. You did well."

"Here, eggnog with a shot of bourbon."

"Well, I'm really not suppose–oh, what the heck." Taylor accepted the beverage, took a sip, then almost gagged. "Oh I see, you put a shot of eggnog in with the bourbon. Good Lord, woman."

Kaylee laughed. "Come on over here by the fire."

The two settled in front of the fire and sipped their beverage.

"You know," Taylor began, "in a couple of hours it will be Christmas day. I have to be honest with you and say that there's no place I'd rather be right now than with the finest company in a warm, toasty house, snow on the roof, and a fire in the fireplace."

"I wholeheartedly agree. Taylor, you have brought a light into my life that I thought could never exist again. I have found in you a friend I can trust, and a person I can rely on." Kaylee looked down. "It's been a long time."

Taylor just stared into her eyes for a moment, moved their drinks out of the way, then he slid over next to her.

"What are you doing?"

"Thanking you for putting up with me for the last week, and…wishing you a Merry Christmas." Taylor then leaned in to Kaylee, and their lips met. No, it wasn't just an ordinary 'under the mistletoe' kiss. There was some meaning behind this one from both sides. The passion had been simmering for the past week.

The fire crackled, burned down a bit, and Taylor was trying to decide whether he should make another trip out to the wood pile, or if he should declare it a night and try to get home through the inclement weather.

He stood up, straightened his clothing, then looked out the window and exclaimed, "Lord, if I don't start for home now, I'll never make it."

"Oh no you don't," Kaylee announced as she closed the fireplace doors. "It's terrible out there; beautiful, but terrible."

"Oh, a lot like you, huh?"

"Hey!" They both laughed. "No, it's just too slick out for you to be traveling. You'll stay here for the night." Kaylee unplugged the tree.

"But you only have one bed. I guess I can camp out here in front of the fire."

"No, you take the bed."

"That's not fair to you. What will you do?"

"I'll be there as well."

It took a few seconds for her statement to sink in, but Taylor finally deciphered her message. Kaylee made sure her message was received by sliding her arms around Taylor's neck and giving him one of the most romantic kisses he ever experienced. He returned the gesture. Taylor then hugged her for a moment, and they stared into each other's eyes. Then the two turned towards the hall, hand in hand, and Kaylee led the way.

Chapter 5

**Wit and Wisdom**

*"If music be the food of love; play on."*

~ William Shakespeare

Anyone who was familiar with Kaylee and Taylor sensed that there was something different about them after the holiday. Whether dealing with them separately or as a team, it was obvious that their dispositions had changed, and for the better I might add. They took this time, the week between Christmas and New Year's, to evaluate their situation with the band and its progress.

We all got together over at my place for New Year's Eve. We had a great time. Taylor and Kaylee couldn't leave the old Mistletoe alone that I still had hanging up. Just before midnight, Taylor made a toast.

"To the New Year; may she be filled with adventure, teach us a great deal about ourselves and each other, and allow us to fulfill our dreams."

Everyone thought the salute was fitting, so we all clinked glasses, drank up, then waited for the clock to pass the high hour. I figured this would be an interesting year, with Taylor being around and all, but little did I know how prophetic his toast would prove to be.

When the holidays ended, the fun and celebration came to an abrupt halt. It always does. It seems that everyone has to do a one-eighty, and get right back into a work mode, often the very next day.

I had enough to keep me busy, but for Taylor and Kaylee, their task to field a proper band had just begun.

From anyone's point of view, the drive to thrive was a giant success. Taylor, however, was still stuck on his 'ten times' total, and the band was barely halfway towards that goal in pledges.

They decided to stick with what worked, however. Taylor would hold court in the music room and try to infuse himself with the student body, and Kaylee would see how much this venture was going to cost the school. You see, putting a band out on the field was only half of the battle. Somehow, they would have to figure out how they could afford new uniforms for the additional members, how they would transport the group to and from each event, and what type of on-field formations would befit a band of one hundred and forty, and growing. Neither of them was used to numbers such as these, at least, not in recent memory.

Now with Taylor, an interesting metamorphosis began to take place between him and his students. It may have been his haircut that earned him additional respect, or perhaps it was a softening of his soul from the effect that Kaylee's love was having on him. Regardless, Taylor was becoming a person people wanted to be around. I believe the term that describes that is 'charisma.'

Students were developing a trust and respect for Taylor, and in doing so, more than a few of them began bringing their problems to him in hopes that the wisdom of this older man, coupled with his understanding of the teenaged soul, could find a solution that only life experience could bring into the mix.

One day, Taylor had a girl come to him after school. Only he and a janitor were in the room at the time. Anyway, the student came to the door and knocked shyly.

"Come on in," Taylor bellowed, in sharp contrast to the girl's reserved persona. She did, and Taylor asked, "What can I do for you?"

"Um, I'm Kathy, and I was thinking of, you know, of maybe checking out the band and seeing, um, if there was some place…"

Her voice trailed off. Taylor took pity on the girl who simply ran out of words. She just silently stared at the floor.

"Come over here, Kathy. Have a seat. Now tell me, do you play an instrument?"

She sat down. "Yes, the clarinet."

"Excellent. Of course, we have room for a clarinet. The more the merrier. Have you ever been in a marching band?"

"I was in the band up until eighth grade, but no, I've never marched and played at the same time," she said while still looking down at the floor.

"Well, we can take care of that. We're going to begin practicing some in the spring, then in early June we'll start marching for real. Sound okay?"

"Yes, I suppose so."

Taylor still wasn't convinced of the girl's commitment. "Is there something else? I mean, you seem a little bit hesitant."

"I want to join, you know, but I just don't want, I mean, I can't deal with…"

Taylor could tell Kathy was tearing up a bit. "You can't deal with the negative reactions from some of the others when it comes to joining the band? Is that what concerns you?"

"Yes."

"Well let me tell you…"

Kathy interrupted him. "It's just that I'm not very popular as it is, and, well…"

Taylor returned the favor by cutting her statement short. He already knew where she was heading with it. "Kathy, there are a few of the football players who are joining up, and one or two from the basketball team as well. The football players will play during half time, then strap it back up and play football before and after the half. Look Kathy, you'll be in good company," he stated. Then, beefing up his enthusiasm, while spreading his arms wide, he declared, "Plus, this band will be the biggest thing to hit this town in fifty years, and you'll always be able to say some day that you were a part of it. How about that, huh?"

"That sounds good."

"You know, Kathy, you can't please everyone, especially your enemies. Your enemies shouldn't concern you, and your friends will always accept you. All in all, you have to be your own person. You're the only one you have to please. From the cradle to the grave, you're it. You're all you've got." Taylor smiled slightly. "I'll tell you what; let me pass on a story to you that I heard many years ago. That might put things in perspective. You've heard of Winston Churchill, haven't you?"

She perked up, for history was a favorite subject of hers. "Oh yes, the Prime Minister of England during World War II."

"Very good. Give the girl an 'A,' Taylor said, looking towards the janitor. "Now in his youth, Winston was quite an athlete. One day he was walking along the banks of the Thames, when he heard another boy crying for help. I guess the other boy wasn't a very good swimmer and was in trouble. Well, young Winston, showing no concern for his own life, dove in and swam over to the lad. The other boy was in a panic and was fighting Winston's attempts to rescue him. It took quite an effort for Churchill, but he finally got the boy over to the shore. Once on dry land, they both collapsed, and Winston finally asked the boy what he was doing out there if he couldn't swim. Well, the other boy began rambling on in another language, which the educated Churchill recognized as German. Through it all, Winston was able to make out that the boy was thanking him for his efforts. Do you know who that other boy turned out to be?"

"No, who?"

"None other than a young Adolph Hitler."

"No!"

"Oh yes. So, do you know what the moral of this story is?"

"Um, I don't know; keep your friends close, and your enemies closer?"

"Oh, very good, but no. The moral of this story is not to believe everything you hear." Taylor smiled.

"So what you just…"

"What I'm saying is, from here on out, use your own common sense and decide what's best for you, because if you spend your time believing everything people tell you, you might begin to accept it as fact." Taylor's eyebrows remained raised.

Kathy looked at Taylor and realized that she had just learned a very valuable lesson. She smiled, held her head up and declared, "I'll be here."

Despite the bright spots, not everything was going smoothly, however. As spring approached, Taylor decided that he wanted to buy the band a bus to transport their equipment. A noble gesture, he thought. Kaylee convinced him to get the students to have a hand in the effort.

"You just can't go around throwing your money at every project and buying peoples' approval. Unless they work for it and have a stake in the outcome, how are they going to learn the lessons that being part of an organization can teach?"

Taylor was used to making things happen so much quicker. "In the day, we would land a contract, record the music, press the discs, get our airtime, do the promos, concerts, all in a six to eight month period," he explained. "I'm not used to doing things on such a small scale."

They came up with a solution, though. They held a few bake sales, raffled off several donated items, and did several 'split the pots' in the lobby during the remaining basketball games. Even though Taylor was frustrated by the process, saying that they were just earning nickels and dimes, they actually came close to raising the necessary funds.

Then as luck would have it, a firm in town heard of their plight, took pity on the organization, and accepted the payment for a fixer-upper bus, while donating the balance. That poor old bus had seen better days to be sure, and I'd be willing to bet the organization actually made money on the deal judging by the poor condition of the bus compared to the amount of money the band had raised. The vehicle, however, was at least safe, intact, and anything that needed repairing was worthy of repair. Taylor had planned to do the bodywork on it, until Kaylee convinced him to let someone else join in the effort. She not only wanted this to be a school-wide effort, she saw how thin Taylor was spreading himself. She worried about him, as he wasn't as young as he once was.

Mr. Spivey, from the auto shop class, grabbed a few of his underclassmen and 'volunteered' them for the project. He was that way. No one had the guts to say no to him. He was built like a fire plug. Mr. Spivey located a local auto body shop who agreed to repaint the exterior royal blue, free of charge, if the bodywork was complete and it was primed first.

As spring approached, Taylor became frustrated with the dwindling numbers the recruitment effort was producing. Be that as it may, the current membership was now an impressive one hundred and eighty-eight band members–more than the school had ever seen– but Taylor still wasn't satisfied. For a while, he said, "We've got to do better." Now though, his words were, "What the hell. I'm just kidding myself here."

To vent his frustration, one day Taylor showed up at the auto shop at the far end of the school and began sanding away at the old, faded paint. He didn't want to wait for the shop boys to begin on it. At least this way he felt as if he was doing something constructive.

The entire bus had to be stripped down, as it had several coats of bucket-and-brush paint over the original school bus yellow. Apparently, this vehicle had transported not only children to and from school, but it also served at least two churches, and some non-conformist group of one kind or another.

The room was cold, the air smelled of lacquer paint, and the lighting was less than ideal. It didn't matter to Taylor. He would sand for a while, then take a break and 'cough up a lung,' as he put it. He didn't have access to the heater and light panel until some of the members of the auto class heard the commotion and showed up to see what was happening.

"Hey, you're the rocker dude, aren't you?" asked some guy they called Curly. Actually, like his Three Stooges counterpart, Curly sported a shaved head, but I'm guessing that he must have had curly hair at some point in his life.

"That I am. Come on in and grab a sander. We're going to take this baby down to the bare metal.

"Man, that's our class work. Are you going to do our homework for us as well?"

"If that's what it takes to get one of you to join the band, then I'll take a shot at it."

"I don't know about that. I mean, I played the drums years ago, but I wasn't near as good as you."

"I don't need you to be as good as me. The world already has one of me. The band needs one of you."

As the work picked up, Taylor continued to regale the crowd with his tales of performing with Vulture, and tailored the stories depending on the audience he was addressing. Some days there were just shop students in attendance, while on the weekends, the place packed out. Needless to say, the stories about the groupies tended to grab the guys' attention, while the glitz and glamour of the spotlight interested many of the female students.

When Taylor first began with this project, I think many of the regulars began showing up on a consistent basis, but then their friends began tagging along. The word began to spread and the sessions became contagious. More people were there to hear Taylor hold court than were there to dirty their hands on the bus. That's what Taylor predicted, and that's what happened. That was okay.

Now, the more he talked, the more students began showing up to work on the bus. One time, the room was packed, and that was funny to see because there were almost more workers than there was work. They resembled a group of ants wrestling over a large crumb. There were people from the auto class working on the engine, several students were on dollies inspecting and repairing the bus's undercarriage, there was about a dozen people at any one time working on the interior, and Taylor and the rest concentrated their efforts on the vehicle's exterior.

Oh, people worked on the bus all right, but Taylor was the main attraction. He would weave his stories of meeting members of The Rolling Stones, The Who, and any other big time musician from that era, into the working session. Of course, many of these names were ancient history to most of these kids, but it was a history they were at least familiar with. Many of those bands were still getting air time, and it was, after all, rock and roll.

It was different when Taylor and I grew up. You see, back in our day, our parents were still attached to the music of the big bands from the 1940s and early 1950s. They thought Glenn Miller, Artie Shaw, and Tommy Dorsey were it. But those characters carried no relevance to us and our generation, because we were into Elvis, The Beatles, and James Brown. There were no cross-over artists from our parents' generation to ours. But in this day and time, many of the kids could at least 'get into' the musicians from our era. While the Stones or the Eagles might not be their first choice when it comes to music, most kids of today can at least appreciate the music and recognize the fact that if it wasn't for these innovators, there might not be any rock music as it has evolved today.

By the time the day was complete, most of the dusty and dirty students left satisfied and felt as if they hadn't even worked a lick. Some hadn't, but the majority had, and yet they still regarded these get-togethers not as work sessions but as B.S. conferences, if you will.

Anyway, like I said, on this day, the room was at capacity, and the situation just grabbed Taylor. "Either you seize the moment, or the moment seizes you," he once told me, "so long as you recognize the opportunity and don't squander it."

Taylor's followers had all taken a seat anywhere they could find a place to sit. It didn't matter whether it was on a bus fender, a bucket, or a tool box. A few were sitting in the bus and hanging out of the opened windows. They had just finished the pizza Taylor had sprung for, and now everyone gathered to hear Taylor's sermon and his bits of wisdom.

When asked what his secret to success was, Taylor told them, "Just act like you know what you're doing, and people tend to accept you and leave you alone." Then he looked towards one of the male students who had been mouthing off in negative tones all day, just trying to get Taylor's goat. "Let me ask you, Craig, have you ever heard of an old-time entertainer named Jimmy Durante?"

"I guess so. Wasn't he some old man on TV with a big nose?"

"At one point in time he was, but amongst his more positive traits, he was an old song and dance man from way back. As I remember seeing him on TV, he wasn't what you would call handsome, dashing, or debonair, to coin an old-time phrase, like most of those in that profession were during that time. But he always went over well and do you know why? Because he believed in what he was doing. He enjoyed himself as well because his song came from his heart. You could see it in his performance. He was himself and didn't let anyone tell him any different. He lived a long, happy life, and most importantly, he was a true success. So you can *do* what you want," Taylor said as his voice hit a crescendo, "and *be* what you want in the time you're allotted here on this plane, and the hell with what everyone else thinks," he proclaimed, then concluded with a quieted delivery, "or you can live a miserable life, conform to the standard, and regret those lost moments for an eternity."

"Have you lived a happy life, Taylor?"

"Well, of cour…hmm." Taylor stared at the ground for a few moments.

"It's a yes or no question, and I think we all know the answer," the young man said as he looked around at his fellow students.

After much hesitation, Taylor realized the guy had him in checkmate, so he did the only thing he could; he answered him. "Look folks, I'll be honest with you. I've made about every mistake a person can make, but I found my way, and I did it the hard way. I chased away every woman who showed any interest in me, and I slept through a good portion of the last decade and a half. Let me be a lesson to you. You can do like me and sleepwalk through life, or you can give it 110 percent and let the chips fall where they may. Growing to a spiritual maturity is never an easy process, and no one has yet to escape from this life without a scratch. But you know what; it's not over for me yet. I believe I've finally found my calling, I think, and it's with you guys. If I can motivate just one of you, if I can send you on the right path in life, then yes, I will have lived a good, happy life. It's only beginning for you. That's the answer to your question. The choice is yours, the choice is mine."

Taylor then waded into the crowd and stated, "Folks, let me tell all of you something. I'm going to teach you a thing or two here. Back when I was playing with Vulture, some of our songs were incredibly nonsensical, but we played them with such intensity that we had people believing that we were experiencing another realm of reality, you know, like some of those opium-induced artists who painted those bizarre paintings. People would gaze upon them and think that they were brilliant pieces of work because, quite simply, they didn't understand them. And if they didn't understand them, the artist must be on a higher level than the rest of us, right? Hah, reality; most of our songs were just album-fillers, and many surrealistic painting merely throw the label of 'creativity' at their project as a way to cover for a lack of any real talent."

One student asked, "Taylor, are you faking it now?"

With a shake of the head, he replied, "I've never been more serious in my life. I don't have the time to B.S. anymore."

At the final break of the day, Taylor's educational session kicked in once again. One of the students changed gears and asked Taylor about his band, wondering how they had all managed to get along through the years.

"We've all heard the stories of The Beatles' nasty break up and all."

"Well, with us, it was cool at first, Vulture, but towards the end, we just got on each other's nerves big time. That happens a lot in the business. I mean, there are creative differences between the members, especially when you consider that you spend ten to fourteen hours closed up in a studio playing the same song over and over and over, and your buddies still can't get the notes right. It gets to you after a few years. You all don't have to worry about that though. You're only here for a short spell, and you have to hit it big, like right now. There is no tomorrow."

Then, the mood overtook him, as it did occasionally, and acting the part of a preacher, Taylor stood up, waded through the crowd, and proclaimed, "Let me tell you folks, music teaches. If you understand music, you will understand life. There is a correlation. Follow me here. Music brings the notes together to form a song, okay? And music brings people together to play the notes. Those people join together to form a band. Yes, people do their own thing with their instrument of choice, yet at the same time through their performance, they all try to become part of the whole. What ends up being produced is a symphony to our ears, and a work of art to God's heart. And that, my friends, is life. We are each a piece of living fabric that makes up the quilt of humanity, and in a band, each instrument plays for the good of the whole, and in turn, for the benefit of the masses."

Taylor was not only inspired, but inspiring. He was really on a mission. He spread his arms wide and continued in a louder voice. "In the early, formative years of the band, for that brief shining moment when you realize that you're on to something special, I mean *really* special, you have your pen in hand, you feel the planets lining up, you watch the notes as they drip on to the paper, and you see everyone and everything coming together, well let me tell you," he said as his head nodded slowly three times, "there's just nothing like it." His voice briefly raised another decibel as he completed his sermon in a near shout. "You hear the gates of heaven open up and the angels rejoicing, for they recognize that a heavenly notion has transformed itself from a spiritual design to a physical reality." He slammed his hand down on the table, and the sound echoed off the cinder block walls. "That's what it's all about, my friends."

"Wow."

"Wow is right!"

The students enjoyed listening to Taylor. It was like being around one of their peers, except he looked a little bit like their grandfather. They learned quite a bit about music in Taylor's presence, but they learned even more about life. And since there were no tests at the end of these sessions, the students seemed to get more out of them. The tests would come later.

When everyone was in the process of cleaning up that day, a girl named Susan, who was a fine saxophonist in her own right, expressed her concerns to Taylor as to why she had hesitated in joining the band. No, it wasn't because of the reaction she would receive from her peers, but apparently her sister had played the same instrument in the band three years prior, and she was one of Mr. Harmon's favorites. Her sister had earned a music scholarship and was entering her final year at Miami University. Susan didn't even want to try because she knew there was little chance she could measure up to what she perceived as her parents' expectations of her.

"Come over here," he told her. "You know, when I was a little boy," Taylor began, "I remember my dad walking by me in the living room one time, and I noticed that the top of my head just came up to his belt. I always thought I'd never grow to be as tall as him. It was impossible, I thought. How could I be any bigger than I am right now? Do you know what?"

"You grew taller than him."

"No, he was six-foot-three the last time I saw him, and I only made it to six foot, but in many ways I stand taller than him. My dad never made more than twenty-five thousand dollars a year, never had people cheering for him, and never wrote a song, or even a poem for that matter. He wasn't very good at expressing himself. You see, it's not somebody else you have to top. You just have to be the best you that you can be. You don't have to be your sister junior. The world already has one of her. They need one of you, and we need one of you." That did the trick as Susan broke out in a smile, and has carried that lesson within her to this day.

Others got along with Taylor the more they were around him. Sometimes it took longer for some to experience his enthusiasm. The idea of keeping Taylor on a full time basis became a bit more palatable to Principal Dooley. Despite the occasional rumor, Dooley wasn't above bragging to his fellow administrators from neighboring school districts on the great find he made with Taylor. Dooley had a right to brag. Taylor had the numbers in the band up over the two hundred mark. Taking a band from twenty-eight members the year before to over two hundred this year–most considered that a miracle.

There was one other person who was taken with Taylor: Kaylee. The two had clearly become an item, an attachment Kaylee was quite pleased with. Taylor, however, had some reservations. You see, he was not quite twice Kaylee's age. While most men would savor a situation such as that, Taylor was still a bit uncomfortable. He wouldn't commit himself one way or another as far as their relationship went. God forbid that one would bring up the 'L' word. Kaylee grew a bit frustrated at Taylor's middle of the road approach, and one weekend decided to pin him down on the subject of 'them.'

"Taylor, how do you feel about me? About us?" she once asked.

"What do you mean? I'm happy to be with you. I love being with you. I'm proud to say that you're in my corner. You're my rock."

"You know, you don't have to be shy about telling me how you feel about me. Girls like to hear those things."

"I know. I guess I never was any good at expressing myself.

"Oh, so you went on to become a song writer?"

"I just mean that I didn't do well with my marriage. At that time, I guess I was married more so to my work rather than to my wife. Out of the blue, she just up and split. She didn't even have the dignity to ask for a proper divorce. She got a quickie divorce in Mexico. To be honest, I didn't really even shed any tears when he she left. I guess I was too preoccupied with work, drugs, and still wanting to enjoy the single life."

"Then you probably weren't truly in love."

"Probably not." Taylor said. "After that, I guess most of my dates were just one shot deals, and before that, my relationship with my mother wasn't very good. So there you go, Albert Schweitzer, figure that out."

Kaylee just looked strangely at Taylor, and despite the seriousness of the moment, she almost burst out laughing. "Taylor, who did you mean to say?"

"That old psychology guy. You know, Albert Schweit-Albert Einstein? One of those Albert guys."

"Did you mean Freud? Sigmund Freud?"

"Yeah, whatever, one of those bearded doctor guys who were always hung up on sex. There I go again. Why do you even want to be seen with someone as dumb as me?"

"Because I care about you. I care for you. I now have to ask why you want to be seen with me?"

"Are you kidding? You're only like a perfect ten."

"Is that the only reason you like to be with me; to be seen with me because of my looks?"

Taylor's voice quieted. "Okay, it maybe it was your youth that initially grabbed my attention, and while I could be attracted to you like a bee to honey, this is a two-way street. I do care about you, and for you. And you know, you have a say in whether this relationship will be a go despite my age as well. You just said that you cared about me too."

"Are you?"

"Huh? Am I what?"

"Are you attracted to me like a bee to honey?"

Taylor hesitated as he weighed the gravity of what he had just said. He looked up at her, directly into her inquisitive eyes while showing vulnerability in his own. He answered, "Yes. Kaylee, you make my heart dance, and that's coming from a man with two left feet."

She took delight in his attempts to express himself. He didn't trust anyone else with his feelings. And while his statement wasn't an 'I love you,' she considered it a great first step. She at least knew where he was coming from, and perhaps where they were going.

This winter was turning out to be a great time for Taylor and Kaylee. The band membership was increasing, they had acquired a bus, and the two had fallen in love. It wasn't all beer and skittles, as they used to say, but they were learning each other's strong points and weaknesses. A disagreement did arise when they began looking into acquiring new band uniforms. Taylor wanted to cut a check for the entire lot to avoid the hassles, but Kaylee disagreed.

"You can't just use your money to 'buy' a band for the school. The members, their parents, and the others within the school have to be a part of this movement. We've been through this all before. Like it or not, those are my rules."

"You're awful bossy all of a sudden."

"Someone has to give this out-of-control ship of yours a rudder."

Taylor just shrugged and walked away. He knew she was right, but he was still used to be the one putting in an order, then having it filled. That system was a lot less bother, but he had to be reminded that he didn't start out that way. He got to that point through many years of hard work, and a break or two along the way.

This entire experience, the organization of the band, teaching and being around young people, and returning to his roots, invigorated Taylor. It had been some time since he had been able to look at himself in the mirror and not be repulsed by the man looking back.

Towards the end of March, the weather turned unseasonably warm. That's not unheard of in the Ohio Valley, but it is always welcomed. Taylor walked around the parking lot of the school with his arms outstretched, just feeling the warmth of the sun against his skin, and he realized that these few seasonal reprieves were to be cherished. No one amongst us knows how many of these we'll be allowed to enjoy from here on out, so it is imperative that we take advantage of them.

Taylor decided to knock off early and go somewhere. He had no idea where, but he just needed to get out and about. He didn't golf, although today would have been ideal for the sport. He really didn't exercise either, but he should. Finally, he figured he would get to where he was going a lot quicker if he actually began his journey as opposed to just thinking about it.

Taylor jumped in his car and began to drive. Yes, there was still a residual winter nip in the air, but he rolled his window down nevertheless. He crossed over the river that divided the town into its east and west sectors, then drove through the downtown business section. He was stopped at a light when a man carrying a bundle of flowers approached his car.

"Hey buddy, how about some flowers for the missus?"

"No, that's okay."

"Oh come on; a handsome fellow like you must have a real pretty gal somewhere, not to mention a wife at home." The man cackled a dry laugh. "At ten bucks a bundle, you can't do that good at a florist."

"Picked fresh from your garden this morning, huh?"

"There you go," he said, followed by another laugh. "How about it, buddy?"

Taylor thought for a moment, then before the light changed, he whipped out his wallet, handed the man a ten spot, grabbed the flowers, then watched as the guy hobbled back across to the corner where he had a bucket holding several other bundles of flowers. Taylor now knew where he was going to go.

The light turned green, and Taylor made a beeline for the turn lane. He made it without cutting anyone off, turned left, then headed down Greenwood Lane. Taylor entered the cemetery through the over-sized wrought iron gates, then drove over to Section X. He parked the car, got out, and walked in the direction of Lenny and

168

Ellen's headstones. A few old leaves left over from last fall remained in pockets on the ground, but Taylor kicked his way through them.

The immediate area had changed a bit since Taylor was last out there. Thanks to the changing seasons, the ground was no longer parched and cracked. The area surrounding their plots had been filled in and reseeded, and it was already showing promises of new growth.

Like his last visit, Taylor just stood and looked at the two stones in front of him, but this time they appeared in a different light. Maybe it was the absence of the hostility Taylor brought with him last fall. Maybe it was the break in the weather itself. It was always possible Taylor's structured environment had him seeing life in a new way. Perhaps it was his sober attitude towards life in general. It didn't matter. While Taylor didn't say anything during this visit, it was what he didn't say that counted.

Taylor bent down and laid the flowers between the two stones, then straightened up. He placed his hands in his pockets, and after a few moments, he turned and strolled away.

April 4th rolled around, and as is customary at that time of year in this area, Opening Day for baseball welcomes in the warmer weather and happier times. We take this occasion to celebrate the conclusion of the winter freeze, and we begin anticipating a summer filled with swimming pools, sunshine, and ice cream cones.

I was fortunate enough to land two coveted tickets to the big game, and asked Taylor if he would like to go.

"Come on, guy, you've been pushing things a bit too hard. You need a little get away time."

Taylor had never attended an Opening Day game, so he agreed, and the two of us drove to Cincinnati to watch the Reds take on the New York Mets. The atmosphere is always electric for that game. I can't recall when the first game of the season for baseball's first team wasn't standing room only.

Taylor and I had to park quite a distance and walk through the downtown area on our way to the ballpark. We crossed the four lanes on Main Street to get to the walkway where we could access the park's entrance.

During out three-block journey, we encountered many vendors hawking their wares including jerseys, caps, and traditional baseball foodstuffs of all kinds. Along that same avenue were those asking, or begging to be more precise, for funds for just about anything you could name. A few of the down-and-out sported signs announcing to the world their disabilities, while at the same time requesting donations of any size. A few others were willing to sing for their supper, quite literally, as they brought their instruments with them for an impromptu concert.

One young man grabbed Taylor's attention. This African-American youth brought several five-gallon buckets with him and had set up shop. He sat on one, had another in front of him for donations, and rested a third between his legs as he beat out an unbelievable rhythm that would have rivaled many professional drummers. He could carry a beat. Taylor recognized the young man; it was Jamaal.

"Hey, Tay," I began, "let's grab some peanuts out here. They're cheaper than inside."

"You go ahead. I have some business to tend to out here."

I looked at Taylor funny, but then spotted a former colleague of mine, so I reintroduced myself to this long lost friend while allowing Taylor to do his thing.

Taylor approached the fellow with the bucket. "Jamaal, isn't it?"

Jamaal momentarily ceased his drumming. "Man, if you want to talk, it will cost you. Time is money, you know."

"That it is. What the hell are you doing down here? You're supposed to be in school."

"So are you. School's for losers, man, and that's where you belong." Jamaal then used the two sticks to form the letter 'L' and aimed it in Taylor's direction indicating that he was a loser. "I can't make no money up there. I can clear twenty dollars an hour here, so keep on moving. You're cutting into my earnings."

"If I give you ten dollars, will you listen to me?"

"Sure, sellout. Bring it on."

"Sellout?"

"Hell yes. You sold out. Look at you; you're not yourself. You cut your hair so you would be like everyone else and they would like you, man. That's a sellout."

"I cut my hair because my girlfriend likes it like this."

"So, then you sold out to someone else. Either that or you're whipped. Same deal."

With that, Taylor wrestled the bucket away from Jamaal and shouted out, "Okay folks, step right up. Let's get this young man here some money so he can go to college! He can't spend the rest of his life sitting on his ass out here on the streets. That will cost you as taxpayers. Let's help him out and have him be a positive force in this world rather than a burden to society. Let's go!"

Taylor then kicked the donation bucket out in the middle of the sidewalk and began beating out a rather fast-paced drum solo on the bucket, and that attracted a crowd. Taylor was giving it his best effort, and to be honest, I don't think he had played like that in some time.

"Yeah, yeah, give him a hand up, not a hand out!" Taylor shouted as he continued his solo. I'm sure I heard the beat of a Vulture hit song *The Burnin' You're In* somewhere in there as his hands became a blur. It was working. Taylor easily passed the ten-dollar mark, but continued on for a spell to hammer the point home to Jamaal. Taylor finished up with a three claps of the sticks on the bucket, and applause rang out amongst the crowd that had gathered. "Thank you and enjoy the game."

Taylor bent down and scooped up the money. He counted it quickly as accuracy wasn't important at this time. "There you go," an out-of-breath Taylor said. "Almost twenty-five dollars. Beat that, schlep."

"Man, what was all of that about?"

"I wanted to show you that you're not as good as you think you are. You've been out here for over a half hour I'm guessing. How much have you earned, ten dollars?"

"Maybe."

"Yeah, maybe. I doubled your take in less than five minutes."

"Big deal; so you're better than me. Is that all you wanted to do? Embarrass me and run my ass in the ground? Big man."

"No, but I did want to talk. Jamaal, I was hoping to convince you to join the band."

"Are you kidding? A high school band? Are you for real, man?"

"Why not? You obviously can't make it on your own. Ten or twenty bucks on game day will hardly pay for your gas just to get down here."

Jamaal began to say something, but Taylor interrupted him.

"Jamaal, no one's expecting you to become a doctor or a physicist or anything above and beyond what you're capable of being, but you're going to be a senior next year and it's time to commit yourself to something in your life other than just goofing around. A senior; man, you've got school whipped. You own the place. You're top dogs as seniors. That's a privilege I never was able to enjoy. It's now or never. Stretch yourself and see what you're capable of doing with what you've been given in life. Start here. Just do something!"

Jamaal listened impassively. He tried to say something, but he wasn't sure where to go with his thoughts. "Man, I don't, I mean, I'm not sure where…what…"

"You don't have a clue about your path in life right now, do you?"

"I have dreams just like everyone else," he shot back.

"Dreams are for those who sleep through life, as they say. What are your plans?"

With a mixture of anger and sadness, Jamaal just looked towards the ground. About that time, I walked upon the scene.

"Let me tell you something, J, I've seen your transcripts. You're good at math. Very good in fact, therefore you understand how all music can be broken down into a numerical pattern, you know what I mean? That's how you're able to become such an outstanding drummer. You understand it, man. You know what it means to have four beats per measure in four-four time. Look, I wasn't much at school. To be honest, I dropped out before I graduated, a fact I'm not too proud of. But you see, I'm blessed with the same gift in math that you are, and yet you have so many more options available to you than I was afforded. You can use that gift of yours for drumming…or engineering for that matter. It's up to you. You can do it if you want," Taylor said as he looked skyward, "or you can sit on a street corner and beat a God-damn bucket until you're a little old man with blistered hands and empty pockets. Beat a bucket, then kick the bucket. Is that what you want on your headstone? Not too much to be proud of, is it?"

Taylor struggled to his feet, then handed the sticks back to Jamaal. "You can do it." Taylor began to walk away, but then he turned back towards Jamaal, pointed, and repeated his statement to emphasize his point. "You can do it."

As we continued our walk towards the ballpark, Jamaal resumed his drumming. I said, "I didn't know you had been granted access to the students' transcripts."

"I haven't."

"You B.S.'ed him?"

With a shrug, Taylor replied, "I encouraged him."

As we turned the corner, I commented, "Man, Tay, you really lit it up on that bucket. I'll bet it's been years since you've drummed like that."

Taylor, walking with a bit of a hobble replied, "I think I tore my shorts."

Be that as it may, Taylor had done all he could with Jamaal. He had planted the seed and hoped that nature would take its course.

There were times, however, when the student became the teacher and taught Taylor a lesson or two. Such was the case later in that same month when band membership had hit another lull. While he was grumbling about it to the chorale director, Kevin McDonald, Taylor found himself with an unusual situation when a student wanted to get her brother in the band. The two knocked on the door while Taylor was reviewing some uniform prototypes that had been dropped off earlier in the week. He was asking Kevin his opinion of the design choices.

"Come on in. What can I do you for?"

The girl, Leslie, had a request. "Hi Taylor, this is my brother Jeff. He would like to join the band."

"He would, would he? Great!" Taylor got up, walked over to Jeff and presented his hand. "Jeff, how are you doing?"

Shyly, Jeff shook Taylor's hand and answered, "Fine." That's when Taylor sensed something different about the student. Leslie noted Taylor's change in perception.

"Taylor, Jeff is a mentally challenged student and is in the special education program here at Hamilton. He does well around others, but still has a few degrees of difficulty."

Taylor showed obvious skepticism, but wanting to be fair said, "Well I'll tell you what, he can audition for me and we'll see what he can do."

Taylor walked over and sat down next to Kevin, whispering out of the side of his mouth, "And you thought I wasn't having trouble recruiting new members."

Jeff removed his trumpet from the case and fumbled with the mouthpiece a bit. Leslie snapped it in place, whispered words of encouragement to Jeff, then stood to the side.

Jeff put the horn to his lips, and once he was ready, proceeded to play his trumpet skillfully and with the proficiency of a lifer. The notes were crisp, his transition between keys was smooth and precise, and he could carry a tune like few others Taylor had heard. Taylor looked at Kevin, and Kevin raised his eyebrows as if to say, "Wow. What do you have to say now?"

Taylor heard the student out, and Jeff finished with a playful little eight note, two stanza folly.

"Wow, the guy can even improvise. Jeff," Taylor said while rising from his seat and grabbing one of the new band hats, "I haven't heard a trumpet played like that in many years. There's only one thing I have to say about that." He then walked over and placed the hat on the young man's head. "Welcome to the band."

Jeff was a fine, if not exceptional addition to the marching band. But there were also those who also tried out for the band, and while they were good, a few of them suffered from their own inner handicaps. One person who comes to mind is a girl named Chrissy. She was a horn player, and while she did fine in a one-on-one audition, when she had to face a crowd, she froze. That was the reason she didn't come out for the band in the first place. She was one of Taylor and Kaylee's recruits.

Taylor tried to encourage her. "This isn't a place to be shy, Chrissy. Let me ask you something; do you remember a rock vocalist way back when named Abby Hunter?"

"I think so. I've heard of her."

"You've heard of her because she actually went on to become a fine singer in her own right. But, in her early years when she came to us to do some back-up for our *Pickin' on Sunset and Vine* album, she was good, but still quite raw. She had a great voice, but she was so self-conscious that she found it impossible to record in front of us. She insisted on a blacked out booth. For the sake of completing the album, we accommodated her. But when the album took off, it was in her contract that she had tour with us for at least fourteen dates."

Taylor then got up and acted as if he was standing in front of a microphone onstage. "When she faced a live crowd, Abby was shaking like a leaf, but I finally told her right before we went on that for this one time, go out and become someone else. Be a–oh I don't know–a singer from Texas who was too good to be seen up on stage with a trashy group such as Vulture, but as a favor, I told her, you're going to lend your voice to us to make us look better. You know, we're all frustrated actors in one way or another. I told her to act like Abby Hunter-headliner, vocalist, hard rocker extraordinaire, who is queen of the stage at any other venue. Act like a singer who owns the audience, I told her, for it's not the audience that owns you. She couldn't be owned, I said. Well, after her first number, Abby just blossomed and came alive. I think that was a turning point in her career, because from then on, she could really belt out a song. It wasn't just the notes she sang, but it was her soul that she put into each song that was now apparent. That was a key to her later success. The rest was history for her, and a good history, if I remember correctly."

177

"Really?"

"Really. Try it. If you think of yourself as someone else initially, someone more experienced, then you will eventually locate the real you inside, and it will take over. Think of that technique as a mental bridge. There is an outgoing musician within you, and when it blooms, you will see who you really are; a complete, total, talented person-body, heart, and soul. That ability is always within you. You just have to find it and bring it out."

"Thanks, Mr. Ross." Chrissy smiled, then got up to leave.

Taylor added one last bit of wisdom. "Chrissy, always keep your fears ten feet behind you, for if you allow them in front, they will lead you."

Someone later asked Taylor if that story he told Chrissy was legit. He just shrugged and walked away.

As April was nearing an end, the strain began to show on Taylor. He was more tired than usual, and Kaylee chalked it up to long hours. She suggested that they do something light that weekend.

"Such as?"

"I don't know. Something fun. We both need to get away for a while and just play."

"Play? Okay, then I'll tell you what, how about if we go to the park, fly a kite, and take along a picnic lunch?"

"Oh my God, Taylor, you're brilliant! That's perfect."

"Do they still make kites?"

Well, they do still make kites, even the old-fashioned kind. They found a diamond-shaped kite and a ball of string at, of all places, the old hardware store over on Main Street. Taylor was grateful, for he didn't think he knew how to operate those 'new-fangled' ones. He yearned for trouble-free times and simpler ways, especially now. To be honest, I think that old Man in the Moon kite they purchased was about as old as the hardware store itself.


"Let go!" Taylor yelled, and Kaylee released the bridle string of the kite. Taylor ran, at least the best he could, and managed to get the kite aloft. Once they had determined that the tail was just right for the wind conditions, they walked over and sat under a tree for a spell, watching the kite fly. Taylor leaned against the trunk while Kaylee leaned against him.

Taylor said, "You know, as a small child I used to be the kite king of Woodward Avenue."

"Sounds like you spent a considerable amount of time alone during your childhood."

"Probably. Sometimes it was my only safe place. Anyway, since I was usually alone, I perfected the one-man kite launch. I could lay the kite face-down on the street, let all two hundred and fifty feet of the string out, then run. Somehow, the kite would float over the roof tops and catch the breeze. Voila! One time, old Mr. Pfeiffer, our neighbor, gave me a huge roll of nylon string and challenged me to get a kite out with that. Looking back, I don't know if he was trying to embarrass me by doing that, thinking that it had to be impossible to pull that off of course, or whether he actually thought I could do it."

"Mr. Pfeiffer? Isn't that the guy whose house you, Dave, and Tom used to toilet paper?"

179

"Yes, they're one and the same. I guess you could say that we had a real love-hate relationship. You see, as we got older, he got meaner. Well, maybe we were the ones that changed. Anyway, back to the kite story. I guess conditions were just right, and do you know, I unrolled that entire ball of string–all fourteen hundred feet of it? It was amazing because the string was so heavy and it sagged so far down, that I had to back up into Mr. Pfeiffer's yard to keep it from getting hung up in the trees down the block. You never stepped foot in old Mr. Pfeiffer's yard, but he allowed it this time. That kite was so far out that some passersby asked me what I was doing. I told them that I was flying a kite, and they had to squint to see that three-foot red diamond hanging in the sky over fourteen hundred feet away. They would just shake their heads and walk away. I don't think they saw the point."

"And what was the point?"

"It's the challenge. If you can do something that most people think impossible, that puts you one up on everyone else."

"It makes you better than everyone else?"

"No, it sets you apart from everyone else. It gives them something to think about, something to shoot for. It gives them something to wonder about. To be honest, I think Mr. Pfeiffer himself was amazed. He later told me I had the kite out over a quarter of a mile!"

"Maybe he had faith in you all along and pushed you to be the best, in a sense."

"Yes, I suppose you could see it that way. Maybe." Taylor looked up at the kite flying effortlessly in the sky. "Looking back, I often felt bad for the way I treated him in my adolescent years, but kids will be kids, you know? We were mean and we were rotten, but

I guess it's not how you get to the finish line so long as you get there."

"And you try to avoid elbowing everyone else in the process."

"Agreed. You know, there were other times when people would walk by and marvel on how I could fly a kite on such a windless day. I could do it, you know. I guess you can always find a breeze if you know where to look. Sometimes you just have to get above it all to…find…your…reward."

The two just look at each other. Kaylee rested her chin on Taylor's shoulder.

After a few moments, Kaylee said, "Tay, I heard a saying years ago that went, 'To get something you never had, you have to do something you never did.' You see, when God takes something from your grasp, He's not punishing you, but merely opening your hands to receive something better. You've received a gift, this band project, and now it's time for you to run with it."

"Yep, but I think I'm running out of gas."

"Oh, but you can't run out of gas. You haven't crossed that finish line you spoke of yet."

"Perhaps, but you know, it seems that once we reach a certain age, we no longer have the steam to finish the race, nor the time to relax and be ourselves. I guess we work too hard and become too busy trying to earn a living to actually enjoy the *process* of living."

"Well, you know what they say: Life is what happens to you when you're busy making other plans."

"Ah, John Lennon. You know how I feel about him."

"And that is?"

"To be honest, I thought he was weird, unlike us other musicians," he said, followed by a small laugh. "By the time I met him, he was at the point in his life where he thought the only good music was a song about what he and Yoko were doing in their relationship. He hated Paul's modern, hip stuff. He thought he was a sellout. He seemed to hate a lot in his later years, and that came from a man who professed so much love and peace to the world. Hypocrites. I guess the scales of human existence have to balance out one way or another. You know, at one time, it seemed that Lennon was only concerned about the happenings of the world. When I met him, he was only concerned about himself. Perhaps he had done all he could do for human kind and thereby had given up on the world."

"Well, then, how about the Byrds. They sang in their song *Turn, Turn, Turn* that there's a time for every purpose under heaven. Your purpose now is to relax. Tomorrow you can jump back on the bandwagon."

"Uh huh." Taylor looked up towards the kite once again. "You know, it seems that once we grow up, we grow old and seem to forget the carefree lifestyle we once enjoyed as children. We didn't have to think about it back then; we just did it. I think our hearts forget. If I could, I would still be running down Woodward Avenue trying to get my kite aloft, eating peanut butter and jelly sandwiches, and catching lightning bugs after dark. But we have to grow up and move on, I suppose. I guess you're right. There is a time for every purpose under heaven. My time now is to work. Time waits for no man, and time marches on, as they say."

"Taylor, look up. Your kite is airborne right now, we have sandwiches here to eat, and if you're a good boy, when we get home,

I'll find you an old mayonnaise jar so you can go out and catch lightning bugs tonight."

"They're not out yet. It's too early in the year."

"Whatever! Taylor," she said with a little exasperation to her voice, "you're blessed right now in that you have the time to do all of that. You've made a handsome living and now have the means with which to break away and do whatever you want, when you want."

"No, I still have things to do, important things, but maybe someday."

The two enjoyed the day, but cut things a bit short as Taylor was still feeling a bit drained. Perhaps the run was too much for the out of shape man. They reeled the kite in, loaded up the car, and returned back to Taylor's place.

Kaylee had Taylor lay down on the couch and told him that she'd get him some aspirin. She went to Taylor's medicine cabinet, opened it, then stopped in her tracks. There were a variety of prescription bottles containing the names of medications she wasn't familiar with. Some of the bottles were new, while others were near the end of their shelf lives. Kaylee was shocked because she didn't know anything was wrong with Taylor.

She did find some aspirin and took two of the tablets to Taylor along with a glass of water.

"Here, you rest. I'm going to play around on the computer a little bit."

Kaylee returned the glass to the bathroom, grabbed the bottles of medication, then booted up the computer to find out what the medicines were and what they were used for. Yes, she knew she was snooping, and perhaps this was none of her business, but she and Taylor were growing closer as a couple, and she felt she had the right to know if something was ailing him.

"Okay, let's see, the first one." She typed in the name Premextred and read the copy. "This drug is usually used in conjunction with Carboplatin. Well, that doesn't help me much." She kept typing.

"Here we go. Premextred: This drug is usually used in conjunction with Cisplatin to treat people with pleural mesothelioma. In most cases, people who receive this treatment are not good candidates for surgery." A cold sweat broke across Kaylee's scalp. She then typed in Carboplatin, and up popped the following description: Carboplatin is a chemotherapy agent used for the treatment of many types of cancers including ovarian, stomach, and lung cancers. She typed furiously looking for a definition for mesothelioma. Unfortunately, she was successful in her quest as the next entry came up:

*Mesothelioma is a form of lung cancer where malignant cells develop in the mesothelium, a protective lining covering most of the body's internal organs. Its most common site is the pleura, or the outer lining of the lungs and internal chest wall, but it may also occur in the peritoneum, the lining of the abdominal cavity, or the pericardium, a sac that surrounds the heart.*

Kaylee just stared at the screen for an inordinate amount of time. She was literally shaking at this point. She didn't know whether to cry or become angry. First she cried, then she became angry.

Kaylee immediately rose from her chair and stomped into the living room where Taylor was nearly asleep on the couch. She wound her arm back and fired the three prescription bottles at Taylor with all her might. The bottles hit their intended target, startling Taylor and bringing him back from his dream world with a shock.

"What the…" was all he got out before Kaylee lit into him.

"What the hell are these?! Do you mind telling me what this is all about?!"

Taylor picked the bottles up and looked at them. He really didn't have to, for he knew what they were.

"Where did you get these? Were you snooping through my things?"

"Don't give me that crap, mister! I know what these are. Just when did you think you were going to tell me you were dying from cancer?"

"Look, I…"

"Look I nothing. You knew you had this all along, yet you still decided to date me and not tell me. You toyed with my emotions!"

"I didn't mean to." At this point, both had been reduced to tears. "I didn't want to be a burden! I've always felt that I've been one giant inconvenience to everyone in my life. My parents sure as hell didn't want me. That's one reason I left home at such an early age. I dragged my wife down to the point where she didn't have the dignity to even say good-bye. The last thing I wanted to be was a burden to you. I care for you, Kay."

"You have a hell of a way of showing it!"

With nothing left to say, Kaylee turned and stomped out of Taylor's townhouse. The two didn't see or talk to each other at all on Sunday. On Monday, Taylor failed to show up at school. Kaylee was concerned, to say the least. She had visions of Taylor saying, "The hell with it," and moving back to California where she'd never hear from him again until his obituary was published in the paper. For all she knew, the shock from their 'discussion' Saturday night might have caused his illness to progress to the point where he couldn't get out of bed this day. After all, his fatigue did hit him all of a sudden, at least as far as she knew. Had she upset him to the point where he overdosed on his medication? She knew that despite their recent discord, she had to check on him.

Kaylee drove over to Taylor's townhouse during lunch and knocked on his door. There was no answer, but the door was unlocked. Kaylee slowly opened the door, stuck her head inside, and looked around. There was Taylor, motionless, on the couch. Kaylee had a difficult time catching her breath. She was shaking as she entered the room, for she feared the worst. She tiptoed over to Taylor. Reaching down, she shook him lightly.

"Taylor?"

She began to panic. She shook him a little bit harder, and he finally opened his eyes. He didn't look well, but Kaylee instantly didn't think his illness was to blame. Taylor's pupils were dilated, and he seemed startled when he saw Kaylee.

Taylor sat upright and rested his elbows on his knees, and just stared at the floor.

"What the hell are you doing here? I thought you hated me," he replied with a slurred speech.

"You didn't show up for work today. What's the matter with you?"

Taylor continued to look down. "I'm sick. You told me that."

Kaylee grabbed Taylor's chin and aimed his head upward. Before he could swat her hand away, Kaylee could tell Taylor's eyes weren't right.

"Are you stoned? What the hell are you on?"

"What the hell do you care?"

"Oh, that's just great. Is that what you want to do? Do you just want to veg the rest of your life away, then have the coroner peel your urine-soaked carcass off the couch when all's said and done? Oh, the tabloids would have a field day with that one, and they would find out, you know that."

"Hey, you yourself said that the Byrds used to sing, "There is a season–and a time for every purpose under heaven." It's my time to die, so leave me the hell alone!"

He began to roll over on the couch away from Kaylee. She grabbed his shoulder and spun him back towards her.

"No! It's finally time for you to be what you were meant to be," she shouted as she poked her finger towards his face. "For the first time in your life, you have people depending on you! They actually look up to you, although why I'll never understand. Right now you epitomize the party junkie mentality that you're trying to eradicate from these students. Even though you regretted never having had a positive influence in your childhood, you're now going to abandon these people the same way that your parents did you. You can curse the darkness, as they say, or light a candle. You can become a stat, or you can count for something! It's your choice. Be who you're supposed to be. Be the Taylor Ross, or Ross…hell, you don't even know who you are, for God's sake! I thought I knew you, but apparently not. Well, you're always telling your students to "just do

something." Now it's your turn. Get busy living, or get busy dying!
Do something!"

"Hey, I already have done everything! God knows I've-I've been
a surrogate father to many of these kids. I've been their sage, their
educator, and for the most part, their baby sitter. I've done my duty,
fought the good fight, and lost. This was a fight where I never had a
chance. I'm tired. Give me a break."

"A break? You've spent the last twenty years of your life on a
break."

"Well then, I guess I failed. I failed you, and I failed the kids.
Now, are you happy?"

"Don't give me that crap! It's not about me being happy that
you've failed. It's your giving up too soon that pisses me off. You're
not done yet with your life's purpose. We all fail in life, Taylor.
That's not the point. It's how we recover from that setback that
defines us as a person. Wasn't it you who asked the students that if
they didn't sell out for their cause, then what was the point? Right
now you've stumbled, and all of the other runners are streaming past
you. You seem quite content to lay there let them do so. You've
trained your entire life for this last race, and now you're just giving it
away."

She looked at Taylor, then walked out. Taylor rolled over and
contemplated his choices.

Several days passed and Kaylee saw no sign of Taylor. Yes, she
was plenty worried. She thought of the scenario she spoke of to
Taylor, of the paramedics having to scrape him from the couch
several days after he passed. That thought made her ill. It had been a
very cruel thing to say, but it was a very real possibility. Kaylee
worried a bit, and cried even more. Even if Taylor was okay, his

time in this world was most likely limited. There was nothing positive to be seen at this point.

I believe it was an unusually hot, hazy Thursday morning when Kaylee, taking a break, looked out of the double doors in the school's hallway and spotted a lone, skinny figure striping the parking lot to resemble a football gridiron. Kaylee cautiously opened the door, almost acting as if Taylor spotted her, he would run away like a frightened deer. She walked down to the parking lot, where she came upon a shirtless, sweating Taylor. He didn't run.

"Decided to rejoin the human race?"

Taylor didn't look up. "I decided to do it for you. I owe you."

"Don't do it for me. Don't do anything for me, Tay. That misses the whole point."

"No it doesn't," he said while stopping his work to make his point. He looked up. "I'm doing it for you because you're the only person in my life who actually cared whether I lived or died. For me that's a rarity. I've been doing for myself all my life; me, me, me. Now it's time to do for others. I'm doing it for you and I'm doing it for them," he said with a nod towards the band assembling over in the upper field. "And if that makes me a better person, well so be it."

Taylor looked up towards the sky, then continued his speech. "I may be a dead man walking, as they say, but those kids have their entire lives ahead of them. Hopefully, they can make something out of themselves. With any luck, I can contribute in some small way."

Kaylee walked over to Taylor, and despite the abundant perspiration draining down his body, she placed a hug on him.

"Tay, I have only one request. Promise me you'll never bail out on me again like you did the other day. That scared me."

"I know. I didn't mean-I just didn't know…"

"I never told you," she began, "but I was engaged to a man once. When I really got to know him, I realized that he loved his drugs more than he loved me. That nearly did me in, because I couldn't compete with that. How does anyone compete with anything like that? I can't play second fiddle to a person in their life."

"You never will. You're always my number one." Taylor took a deep breath, and with a shaky voice stated, "I never wanted to be a burden to you or anyone. I know I've said it before. I would have asked you to marry me months ago, but I knew that I'd just end up placing you in a nursemaid's uniform. That's no way for a young woman to spend the finest years of her life. On top of that, you're too young to go through life as a widow."

"Why don't you let me decide how I want to spend my life? Without giving me any options, you're cutting me out of the decision-making process."

She was right. The two decided to let it rest for a bit, for they had too much to do for the band at this point. The problem of obtaining new uniforms surfaced once again. A decision had to be made and by the first of June. Kaylee organized a series of car washes, three on the same day to be exact, to take place all across town. They would repeat this for the next three weekends, and pray for good weather.

Taylor got the guys together and decided to put on one more concert for the community. This time it would be downtown at the courthouse square during the Hamilton Pioneer Days festival, which was scheduled the weekend before Memorial Day. This time, their performance would be a fundraiser.

Surprisingly, all went well. The weather cooperated for the car washes, and the concert did about as well as expected. Kaylee and Taylor tallied up the money from all of the donations, and they found that they were still short.

"Okay, so far the Schools Foundation donated nearly $20,000 toward the campaign, and local businesses added another $15,000 for a total of $35,000 toward the amount needed. Have you got that?"

"$35,000. Got it." Taylor was writing and clicking away on the calculator.

"The students managed to raise another $15,000 through their many fundraisers, and the Band Boosters kicked in an additional $7,000. Private donors have either given or willed us $8000, and a sale of our old uniforms to Hamilton High School in Southern California brought us another $5000. What do you have as a running total?"

"Altogether we're pushing $70,000."

"That's great, but we're still a little bit short, you know," she said with eyebrows raised. "The uniform company usually charges $350 per unit, but due to the size of our order, I sweet-talked them into giving us a price break and knocking off fifty dollars per unit. With two hundred and sixty people needing uniforms, that leaves us $8000 short. Tay, how are we going to pull that off? The kids are exhausted. The well is just plain dry."

"You know, it's more like $14,000 that we'll need."

"How do you figure?"

"If we fill all two hundred and eighty slots, the cost will be $84,000. We only have $70,000 right now."

"Well, let's deal with the here and now. We're short money and time. The deadline is Monday. What the heck will we do? We'll just have to order what we can with what we have, I suppose."

Taylor got up and began rooting around in his desk drawer. He pulled out his checkbook and walked back over to the coffee table and sat down. He took out his pen.

"What are you doing? Huh uh, no! We agreed that the kids were going to have to do this themselves."

"They've done all they can do! Every business in town is tapped out. There isn't a brownie in Hamilton that hasn't been baked, sold, and eaten. The kids' fingers are all wrinkled from all of the car washes they've put on. They're musicians, Kay, not scrub jockeys. What is your solution?" Kaylee just stared back. "I thought so."

"Taylor…"

"They've got to have uniforms! They've answered the call and are willing to pay the price. What can we do, say, "Thanks for killing yourself all summer, but a few of you we're going to have to send out there naked."?"

"No one's going out there naked."

"Well, what else can we do? Just think of this," he added as he continued to write, "as a donation from a booster, a concerned citizen."

"Oh, Taylor. Wasn't it you that once said that money wasn't the answer to everything?"

"Yes, but in this case it is. We have a deadline to meet. Sorry."

Kaylee just shook her head as Taylor tore off the check and put it in the pile of other receipts. She then rested her chin on her palm. "I guess I'll call the uniform company Monday morning and let them know that the order we sent up to them is a 'go.'"

This was a milestone for the two as everything was stubbornly coming together. The bus was scheduled to be painted and lettered the following week, the uniforms were going to be in process, and the band membership was up and enthusiastic. Both Kaylee and Taylor sat there on the couch and didn't say a word. For Taylor, he thought this would be a great time to take a breather and smile at all they had accomplished. Kaylee thought the lull could be used for a more constructive purpose.

"Tay, I want to talk about us. More specifically, I want to talk about you and your–"

"You know," he interrupted, "this is only phase one. We still have to chart the field formations, then there's–"

"Taylor, please, we–"

He continued to harp on the unprepared aspects of their attempt to bring this concept to fruition.

"The travel schedule. Have we even drawn up a travel–"

"Taylor, we've been avoiding this for too long. We have to talk about your illness!"

"No!" Taylor yelled while throwing the notebook down. The room instantly became silent as Taylor, with his hands on his hips, stared across the room at nothing in particular. After a moment,

Kaylee got up and gingerly placed her arms on his shoulders and walked him back over to the couch.

"Please, do this for me, Taylor. Help me understand. I know you must be scared at your prospects, but I have to know. I need to be able to understand what we're up against here."

After the deep breath he had promised himself just a minute ago, he began. "Okay, the type of cancer I have is called mesothelioma. As I understand it from the doctors, it is most frequently seen in men between the ages of fifty to seventy. It can attack the mucous linings of the abdomen, but tends to gravitate to the sacs around the heart and lungs. Mine has attached itself to my lungs."

"Taylor, what, I mean, how did you get this? When did you know?"

"I was diagnosed early last summer. The damn thing can incubate for thirty to forty years, then make itself known with such force. I had been getting tired a lot, you know, but I just chalked it up to age. Unfortunately, that problem just became more pronounced as the days went by. I developed a raspy cough, but then again, I am, well, I was a smoker. They did all of the tests, then promised me the sun, the moon, and the stars if I did chemo, but the doctor said that it had already begun to metastasize. What was the point, I figured."

"How, I mean, was it from smoking?"

"At first I thought so, but they said that smoking didn't really raise the risk, although I have to admit that I've smoked some pretty wild stuff in my day. They said that a great majority of the people who develop this type of cancer do so from an exposure to asbestos. The only thing I can think of was when my mom left, my dad had me take over all of her household duties, and that included doing the washing. Dad worked in the brake division at the auto plant, so I'm guessing that through handling his clothes, I ultimately was exposed."

"Is that what your dad died of?"

"I don't know what he died of. I do know what I'm going to die of because this crap is basically incurable. You know, the day the doctor diagnosed me was the day I told Jerry I'd do the Letterman show. I had considered myself retired up to that point, but I wanted one last shot in front of the crowds. That's something I would miss."

"I didn't go through that Elizabeth Kubler-Ross model to deal with this kind of thing; you know, the denial, anger, bargaining reaction to this ordeal. I knew I was a goner, so I accepted it right off even though I didn't like it. I figured that there was nothing that I could do to stop it, so I guess I wasn't as religious as I should have been about seeing my doctors and taking my medication."

Kaylee listened to Taylor's explanation, then became very quiet. When she did finally speak up, she said only two words: "How long?"

"I don't know, Kay, but not long. I doubt that I'll see another Christmas." Shifting a bit, Taylor stared at the ground and became a bit introspective. "You know, back when I was a little boy, my mom used to get these catalogues of Christmas cards around Thanksgiving time. She'd sift through them and pick which one she liked the best, then have them stamped with our family's name. I used to spend hours looking at those cards. Most displayed snowy scenes, probably from some mythical New England town, and from some non-descript time in history. Some of the cards carried that glittery snow, you know what I mean, while a few others had a soft, red felt ribbon on the door's wreath. All of the people were walking, hand in hand, children were building snowmen, and a horse and carriage was parked at the curb. I actually came to believe that's what Christmas

195

really was; a dreamlike happiness in an imaginary rural neighborhood." Taylor gave a small laugh at hearing his own description of an unrealistic dream. "I always wanted to go there, just for Christmas if nothing else."

"But last year, I came to know the true meaning of Christmas, and if that's my final experience with that holiday, then last year made up for all of the lonely Christmases I spent up until that point. Yes, we had the snow and the pretty tree here, but it was you who made that holiday special for me. You were the only one who showed me true love on that day, Kay, and that made up for all of the isolation I've experienced here on this plane."

It was all she could take. Kaylee broke down and began to cry, not weep mind you, but she cried. Taylor put his arm around her, then joined her in crying nearly as hard. I think at that point it was beginning to sink in to him that his time was indeed growing short. Maybe he was realizing that perhaps he really had experienced some of that denial that he disavowed.

That was a long Sunday for the two. After the day's revelations, their conversation was limited. The brevity of one's own mortality became apparent to each of them and cast a pall over the rest of the day.

It was a strange day, Taylor later said. It was as if the traffic had stopped, the birds took the day off, and the phone was out of service. Nothing else really registered to us, he said.

Later on, when it grew dark and was time for Kaylee to leave, Taylor asked her to stay. She was relieved that he had asked her, and she would have suggested that arrangement if he hadn't brought it up.

"I suppose we never know how much time we have left, and we should make...the...most...of...it." Taylor finished his sentence in measured tones, then looked up at Kaylee. She stared back at him and nodded slightly.

"Kay, I want you to stay not only this night, but every night."

"Oh well, Taylor–"

Kay, I want you to be my wife."

Kaylee just stared at him in disbelief. His proposal wasn't totally unexpected. In fact, he had mentioned the 'M' word one other time. But with what had gone on during this day, Taylor's request knocked her for a loop.

"Well, should I have kept my mouth shut?"

Kaylee had forgotten. She was supposed to give him an answer.

"No! I mean, yes, yes, of course I'll be your wife!"

Chapter 6

**Comes a Time**

*"Oh yeah, life goes on,*

*long after the thrill of living is done."*

~ John Mellencamp *Jack and Diane*

The month of June was to be a big one for the band. Even though all they planned to do in the Fourth of July parade was march down the middle of High Street, rehearsals had to begin for the parade this month. They didn't have to do much more than play the Hamilton High School fight song, do a few drum cadences, and one or two patriotic numbers, but appearance meant everything for the group. After all, nearly every business in town had some time or money invested in the band.

Taylor and Kaylee still had to decide what numbers the band would perform at halftime during the season. Like always, they only needed to memorize a few numbers, then mix and match them throughout the season to give the appearance that they actually had several shows going at the same time.

Throwing a wrench into the mix was the fact that a Cincinnati television station had caught wind of Taylor's success, and they wanted to do a story on him. Taylor balked at the idea, but they pressured him by showing up every day at the high school and began filming their practices. He eventually felt that to be aloof would raise suspicions, and if people began digging around, they might unearth evidence of his illness. Taylor didn't want anyone to know about that, not yet anyway.

He sat down with the reporter and gave the usual background information of the hometown boy who graced the world's stage, then returned to help out those in need. Needless to say, he toned down the seedier aspects of his background, before and after Vulture. He gave credit where credit was due, mainly to the community, the band members, and especially to 'Ms. Lewis,' as he referred to her. The reporter later hinted at the couple's involvement, but didn't go too far in depth.

Having taken care of that, there were now things of more importance to consider. Taylor had made a proposal to Kaylee, and she had accepted. They now had to decide what kind of wedding to have, where, and when the event would take place. They both decided that simpler would be better than excessive, and sooner was better than later. Every day they waited, they were pushing the clock, unfortunately.

They finally decided on the third weekend in June. That gave them a couple of weeks to plan, such as it was, and they also had band activities to consider. The day of Saturday, June 25th would be the special day. Kaylee always said that she wanted to be a June bride, and now it would be so.

During the period leading to the nuptials, there was something disturbing I noted in Taylor. His health had begun to noticeably fail. Up until now, he had been holding his own. But now he was getting tired more often, especially out at practice. Around home, he wouldn't get up and move around any more than necessary. My God, I thought, it's going too quick. *He's* going too quick. I'm sure Kaylee's thoughts were along the same lines, but sometimes when a person goes through something like that, there's a certain amount of denial that goes along with the situation. Perhaps she didn't see what I saw, or maybe she didn't want to look too closely.

When Taylor's marriage proposal to Kaylee had been accepted, he called the jewelry store on Rodeo Drive and asked about purchasing an engagement ring. He described it to them, the one they had seen in the window six months before, and the store emailed him a few photos of those that matched his description. Taylor selected the ring that Kaylee had so admired in the window. While it was a beautiful three diamond, two carat ring in a gold setting, with his financial means, Taylor could have chosen a ring of any size, but he stayed sensible in his choice. It was very nice, of course, but not 'Hollywood nice,' as some in his old circle would say. He knew Kaylee loved that ring, and had no desire to live in a style above and beyond what she was used to. That just wasn't her way.

A week before their wedding, I asked Taylor if he had purchased a wedding day gift for Kaylee.

"What do you mean 'gift?' We're getting married. I got her the ring."

"I know, but it's customary for the groom to present his wife with a gift on their wedding day." I looked over at Taylor and knew what was on his mind. He bounced his eyebrows three times. "You know what I mean!"

"I didn't say a thing."

"No, but I knew what you were thinking. I mean, when I married Janice, I gave her a single pearl necklace. She gave me an expensive Mont Blanc pen. I still have it, the pen I mean, and come to think of it, I still have her necklace."

Taylor sat there for a moment, then said, "Okay, I'll tell you what, how about if you give me a lift to Elderman's Department Store. I think I know what I would like to get her."

We drove downtown, with the intent of browsing the store for the perfect gift that said 'I love you.' Taylor already knew what he wanted, however. It was just a matter of whether the store carried it.

Elderman's was one of the few remaining upscale retailers left in the downtown area, and yet their prime as a leading economic player in the city probably took place over a decade ago.

Taylor seemed to be a man on a mission as he did his best to surf between the aisles. He almost lost his balance once or twice, but he caught himself and continued on.

We finally entered the stationery department near the back of the store, and Taylor began looking around. He spotted a table full of inexpensive statuettes over in the far corner, and walked over to them in search of his prize. To be honest, I thought he was just browsing, you know, keeping his body busy while he continued to think of the proper gift. I was wrong as I saw his eyes brighten, then he reached for a five inch tall ivory-colored sculpture. It was one of those little figurines that usually carried an inscription like 'World's Greatest...' fill in the blank. The little moppet had its arms outstretched as if offering a hug. This statue carried the saying 'World's Greatest Teacher' engraved on the base. Taylor just stared at it, then I noticed his eyes began to well up.

I had to break the mood and ask, "Uh Tay, are you sure you want to give her that? I mean it's nice and all, but a gift for an occasion such as this must be something truly special."

Taylor stared a bit more at the little guy, then held him close. "Yes, this is exactly what I want to give her."

Who was I to argue? It was Taylor's wedding, and he has always been anything but conventional. Why change now? Taylor paid for the gift, and I drove him back home.

Taylor and Kaylee exchanged gifts the Friday evening before their nuptials. Kaylee presented Taylor with a photo of the two of them taken the day they were in the park flying their kite. The photo was encased in a sterling silver frame. He thought it was the kindest gesture as that photo was their favorite.

Kaylee waited with anticipation for her gift, and Taylor reached around behind the chair where he had hidden it. It was crudely wrapped, as only Taylor could do. He didn't want any help. He was at that stage in his life where he could still do everything, just not very well. Perhaps that was his denial phase, but the paper was white, the ribbon was silver, and Kaylee seemed to appreciate the effort.

She slowly removed the wrapping, not quite knowing what to expect, and finally uncovered her treasure. She stared at it for a moment, as it really wasn't what she had expected. The figurine was more like something one of her students would give her at the end of the school year.

"Well, that's interesting."

"You don't like it?"

"Oh, I like it." Her voice was less than convincing. "I just think it's a, well, a different kind of wedding gift," she said, followed by a small, uncomfortable laugh. Kaylee was beginning to wonder if Taylor's mental wellbeing was slipping along with his physical.

"You may be wondering why I chose a present such as this." Taylor hesitated, as it had always been a bit difficult for him to express himself when revealing an inner part of his soul.

"I thought this was the perfect gift because you *are* the best teacher. I don't mean just in the classroom, but you taught me more about myself in the time I've known you, than I learned in my first fifty-plus years on this plane. You taught me to rely on myself when the need called. You taught me to reach out to others when I was in need. You taught me that I shouldn't feel ashamed about asking for help. You taught me to get up when I've been knocked down, and you taught me that I do have self-worth. But most important, you taught me that I can love, not just you, but me, as a person as well. All of this time, the drugs, the ear-splitting music, and my playing the part of a loner were all defense mechanisms. They shielded me from a harsh world and kept me from being me. Through the lessons you taught me, you allowed me to find who I am, and all I can truly offer you in return is my love, the love that you planted, nurtured, and now cultivated."

Kaylee placed a loving hug on him.

Taylor took a moment to wipe his tears with a shaking hand. They both sat quiet for a moment. Then, he changed the subject, but only slightly. His voice was quiet.

"You know, when I picked this gift out, I was taken back to a time I remembered from the past. My dad had an older brother, about ten years older. They both fought in World War II. It was certainly a different time, but Uncle Ned said that back when they all came back home from Germany, the girls were waiting there for them with opened arms. While that might sound idyllic, it was so only on the surface. You see, many of the soldiers came home with amputations, scars, burns, some walked with a limp, and some were even missing an eye. But you know what?"

'What's that, Tay?" Kaylee asked in nearly a whisper.

"The women welcomed them all home just the same. Those ladies were so hungry for someone to love, and someone to love them back. The men, well, the men were so grateful that a woman cared enough about them to overlook their defects and accept them as they were. Now that's true love. Today, you cared for me, Kay, even with all of my blemishes. And because of that, I so love you.

As Taylor finished his speech, he slowly looked up to find Kaylee in tears. She began to sob, almost uncontrollably, as she dropped down to Taylor and the two embraced and held each other for some time.

Their wedding took place in the nearby town of Metamora, Indiana, a small town about an hour's drive from Hamilton. Taylor chose that particular town noted for its small antique and knick-knack shops not just for its quaint surroundings, but also because some of the scenes from the movie Rain Man were shot there. That was his favorite film.

It was a simple affair, just the wedding party and a few others settled in at the Fireside Inn. I felt a little sad for Taylor as several from Kaylee's family had come to town not only to witness the couple's nuptials, but also to meet Taylor. The other side of the aisle was nearly empty.

I was Taylor's best man, and Kaylee chose her sister Jackie for her matron of honor. The ceremony was simple as well, brief and to the point. The two exchanged vows in front of the huge, stone fireplace in the reception room, then we all enjoyed a nice dinner.

Despite what many might think, the Ross's marriage was anything but a piece of cake. Kaylee had to resign herself to the fact that she was marrying a man whose time on this planet was limited. Taylor, on the other hand, wondered if he was doing the right thing by marrying a woman "who still dotted the 'i's' in her last name with little hearts," as he put it. She didn't, of course, and she hated it when he said that, but no one could argue that there was an age gap to consider in this true May/December romance.

Be that as it may, it was a fine evening, one you hoped would never end for a variety of reasons, but there was no time even for a honeymoon. They had to get back and ready the band for the parade. It goes without saying that dealing with two hundred and seventy-seven members was quite different than the twenty-eight they had to look out for last year.

The fourth arrived on a Tuesday that year. It was a beastly day to say the least. That wasn't uncommon at this time of year. At ten that morning, the temperature was already nearing the mid-eighties, there was little or no breeze, and the humidity was up there as well.

Due to the size of this year's parade, the staging area had been switched from previous years so it could begin in the downtown area, then finish up at the fairgrounds for judging and final dismissal. Since the story of the day was the Hamilton High band, they were chosen to lead off the parade.

Even though the uniforms hadn't arrived yet, and musically the band wasn't as tight as they soon would be, they were a regal site to behold. They were all dressed in a summer-friendly white button-down shirt and navy trousers, and when they all turned the corner at Front and High Streets, everyone lining the courthouse stood and watched as the band began filling in the entire block between Front and Second Streets. Yes, they were a little spread out, but what a magnificent site it was to behold.

While Kaylee and Taylor weren't the parade marshals–lifelong Hamilton resident and World War II hero Elmer Galloway was–the two did ride near the front of the parade on a float. There was no way Taylor could have made the trek on foot at this point. With every passing day, he was becoming weaker.

When the band began to play and progress down the urban thoroughfare, everything else in the parade seemed anti-climactic. It shouldn't be that way, not on the Fourth, but it was, at least from my perspective. I put away my camera and drove on out to the fairgrounds to meet the Rosses and help them tie up any loose ends. The Hamilton band, of course, won a top band award, and it was only fitting. If they had issued an award for the most improved, they would have won that one hands down as well.

Just as we were getting ready to head to the car, the Cincinnati television reporter approached Taylor.

"Mr. Ross, can I have a word with you?"

"Yes, I suppose so."

"How are you doing? I noticed that you didn't walk the parade route this morning."

"No, I'm not as young as I once was, I'm afraid," he said, followed by an uneasy chuckle. None of us were too comfortable with where this exchange was going. It was too much out of the blue.

"Is your health okay?"

"I'm hanging in there. Why?" Taylor figured that he might as well go to the root of this conversation.

"After a tip, an area pharmacist confirmed that you were receiving anti-cancer drugs. Is that true? Are you suffering from cancer?"

Kaylee spoke up. "That's a violation of patient-doctor confidentiality."

"So you admit that it's true. Do you have any additional statements you'd like to make?"

We all just turned and walked away.

"Mr. Ross, I'll have to report this in my story about the band when it airs."

Taylor stopped and turned. "Look, I don't care what you air. If you can live with yourself, then do what you're going to do." We resumed our walk.

"It will be aired this Friday, if you're interested."

Needless to say, that exchange cast a pall over an otherwise satisfying day. Days on the high side would be few and far between for the Rosses, and we knew it. So, for that idiot reporter to ruin the moment was disrespectful at best.

Taylor became depressed as we drove home. He was either deep in thought, or deep within himself. I dropped him and Kaylee off at their house, and let them deal with it. This was their predicament, not mine.

"Okay, what are we going to do? We could sue to stop the story. At least it would buy us some time," suggested Kaylee.

"Hon," Taylor began, then never really finished that statement. "The man isn't saying anything that isn't a fact. We've got to let it go."

"But then what will you do? The board might ask you to step down."

"From what? I'm a volunteer, remember?" Taylor looked away from Kaylee because in his mind, he saw his alternatives dwindling to a scant few. "In case you haven't noticed, I'm getting weaker every damn day. I doubt that I'll even have the stamina to make it through the season if things continue as they have been." Taylor then dropped his head. "I know what I have to do."

"What's that?"

After a deep sigh and a hesitation, Taylor said, "I need you to accompany me over to Bob Harmon's house. I need to speak with him."

"Taylor."

"I have no alternative. He's the only other one who knows how to run the band. I'm not going to make it, Kay, I'm just not going to make it." He buried his face in his hands and began crying. Kaylee just held him.

That afternoon, the two drove over to Mr. Harmon's house, and Kaylee helped Taylor up the steps to the front door. After two rings of the bell, Bob Harmon answered the door and was startled to see the two standing there. At first he appeared to be angered by their presence, but then, for whatever reason, took on a more understanding tone as he opened the screen door and asked, "May I help you?"

"May we come in?" asked Kaylee.

"Um, yes, of course." Bob sensed that something was out of the ordinary as he noted the decline in Taylor's appearance.

They filed into Bob's living room and took a seat. Kaylee sat on the arm of Taylor's chair as she wanted to be as close to him for support as possible.

"Can I get you all something to drink?" Bob asked, trying his best to be diplomatic.

Taylor disregarded Bob's gesture and jumped headlong into his speech. "Bob, I'm sorry I treated you so bad," he said with heavy eyes. "What I did last fall and how I treated you was inexcusable."

"Coming back to apologize, huh? Do you realize all of the problems you've caused me? My good name and a lifetime of work was shot to hell because of your little diatribe."

"I realize that. I'm sorry because I was truly wrong," he admitted with a shaky voice. Kaylee rubbed his shoulder. "I embarrassed you, and myself, in front of too many people. I tried to show you up thirty-five years ago, and I did the same thing last fall. I guess I never grew up. I was still acting like a stupid kid, you know. I've milked a grudge for decades, and I never learned from it. I guess I put anyone who tried to exert their authority over me in the same boat as my dad. And, I hated my dad, you know. I just took it out on you. Please forgive me."

"Well I'll be damned." Despite what Taylor might have thought of Mr. Harmon, he wasn't a man with a hardened heart. Harmon, now misty-eyed, walked over to Taylor and knelt down. "Taylor, I know this must have taken a lot for you to come over here and ask my forgiveness. You have it a hundred fold, for you see you're no less a man for admitting your failings. Of course, we all have short-comings."

Mr. Harmon rose back to his feet. "While you challenged me on my teaching methods and lost, my own son challenged me on my teaching methods, his upbringing that is, and I lost. I didn't listen to him either because I was so damned intent on being the adult and exerting my authority, just as I did back when you confronted me some three-and-a-half decades ago. I should have listened to you back then, and to my son years ago, but I was just so damned bull-headed. I thought if I allowed someone else direct the action, it would make me less of a man, less of a teacher, less of a parent. I always had to be right," he said while slicking his thinning hair back.

"Despite what you might think," he continued, "I gave my all to my music, and yet I still failed, at least in your eyes. I may or may not have fallen short the way you thought I did, but all in all, I think my music was pretty darn good. That's why it hurt so much when I resigned. I didn't fail with my music, I don't think, but I failed with my own son. That hurts more. I lived for my music and my teaching when in fact I should have been just living. I became so wrapped up in my job that I forgot that a person can wear many hats in this life; in fact, we all should."

"Very good. Apparently you did learn a lot."

"Now, but even though Greg lives only twenty-five miles from me, I see him rarely because of it. *Cats in the Cradle*, you know. And to think he went into music education…just like his old man. My boy was just like me," he said, quoting a line from the afore-mentioned song made famous by Harry Chapin. Bob then took a shaky audible gasp as the realization became apparent that important opportunities had slipped away from both men.

Mr. Harmon sat on the couch opposite Taylor and Kaylee. "I guess now he's busy with his own ship. Doesn't have any time or a need for the old man now, you know," he said with a trembling voice. "Through it all, I failed to appreciate the fact that I might be able to learn from others, any others, regardless of their age or status, and pass that wisdom on. I thought I knew it all. Until just now, I never quite understood my son and his attitude towards me, but I think I'm beginning to comprehend it now. It puts me in mind of an old saying by Ralph Waldo Emerson that goes something like, 'Every man I meet is in some way my superior.' How true that is, and I should have been intelligent enough to see that, but I too failed." With a shake of the head, he continued. "It might be too late for me, but you're lucky. You still have many years in front of you to correct your wrongs."

There was a prolonged, uncomfortable silence. It was Taylor's turn to speak, yet he didn't, not right away. Bob sensed something was amiss.

"Bob, I'm afraid that I'm not long for this world. That's why I'm here. I need your help."

"What are you talking about?"

"Bob," Kaylee began, "Taylor is in the final stages of meso...mesthl..."

"Mesothelioma," Taylor said, helping her out.

"What the hell's that?"

"It's a serious and rare form of incurable lung cancer. The television station doing a story on Taylor and the band unearthed that detail. We were going to keep it quiet as long as possible, but the information is going to be made public at the end of the week," she said.

"Oh my God. Oh, I'm so sorry, Taylor," Mr. Harmon said with his hand cupped over his mouth. "I didn't realize. I mean, I figured that you had some health concerns, but I never knew...I'm so sorry. My God, I'm so sorry." Mr. Harmon's tears flowed freely at this point.

The three of them hanged their heads as each came to accept their own vulnerabilities and imperfections. When things settled a bit, Bob righted himself, took his handkerchief in his shaking hand, and wiped his tear-stained face. He cleared his throat, and in a strained voice said, "Taylor, if there's anything you need, anything, I'm more than ready to help you out. As much as I hate to admit, you've brought back a spirit to the band that I've rarely seen in my fifty years of teaching. You've galvanized a community and brought vitality to the organization that I never could. The threads of this musical tapestry you have woven shall intertwine themselves throughout this town for generations to come."

"But Bob, you commanded respect. I'm a fad, let's face it, but you're a teacher. You're..."

"You're a mountain, Taylor. Don't let anyone tell you otherwise. I've been around this business too long not to recognize that. I'm merely a hill. And a mountain can't be a mountain without a valley to accentuate its importance. The contrast between our teaching methods is vast, to say the least."

After a pause, Taylor replied, "I don't know why it has taken me so long to see that you're very wise, Bob, because it has been written that one day the mountain shall lay low and the valley will rise to prominence. This is your time to rise and shine. I need you. More importantly, the band needs you right now."

"Taylor, I can't handle...I mean, there are so many-"

"I'll be out there. You don't have to handle it alone. I'm not ready to step down yet. Hopefully I can last out the season."

Bob began tearing up again. He dried his face one final time, blew his nose, then said, "I'll be out at the field tomorrow at nine o'clock, if that will do. For today, I hope you can excuse me, I really need to visit my son and speak with him…and apologize. I have an awful lot to make up for while there's still time."

"We must be going as well. Bob, thank you for jumping in and helping out; everybody will appreciate your effort. They always have." Bob just smiled weakly.

All three walked to the door, and Kaylee went to assist Taylor down the steps, but he just waved her off. He gingerly made his way down the three concrete steps, then shuffled towards the car.

"My God, it all finally makes sense now; he came home to die," Bob said with a shaky voice as he watched the pitiful sight.

Kaylee responded, "I think you're wrong. I think he came home to live." She was right, you know.

Bob Harmon did indeed show up at the field the next day, and many of the parents and students were stunned and happy to see him. Despite their past differences, things worked out well between the two band leaders. Taylor needed Bob to provide the foot power that was progressively alluding him, and Bob needed Taylor because he knew the rocker possessed the charisma that brought all of the members together in the first place.

At the end of the first day of co-chairmanship, they called the entire two hundred and seventy-seven members together in a circle. Bob announced, "Well, I hope I can help you all out. That's what I'm back here to do. I'm going to help Taylor out because he might miss a few days here and there. Taylor."

Harmon made his statement, then turned his back to the crowd as if doodling on his clip board. In reality, he was trying to shield the crowd from his eyes. He didn't want them to see his lids heavy with tears.

"Folks, you don't know how good you all make me feel, seeing all of you out here, pulling together for the common cause. I have to be up front and honest with you all. I am battling an illness, a cancer, and it might cause me a little weakness here and there, but remember–I'm always with you. I'm in treatment right now, and with any luck, I'll be around for some time to come. Let's not worry about things we can't do anything about. Any questions?" Before anyone had the chance to say anything, Taylor summed up the impromptu meeting. "Good. See all of you back here tomorrow. Great practice, guys."

The crowd was stunned, as they had been handed quite a bit to digest. Taylor wrestled himself from his lawn chair, and prepared to go home and get some rest.

It was a tough week, and true to their word, the television station ran the story on the early portion of their news. They summed up the piece by listing the drugs Taylor was on and the type of cancers they were used to treat. Yes, they sensationalized it. Needless to say, while they didn't make anything up, they left little to speculation.

The word was out, but with any luck, being on the early news, perhaps viewership was minimal and few people saw it. But one thing was for sure, every band member was tuned in. They thought the piece was to be about them, and it was for the most part, but the last little blurb about Taylor's cancer must have floored them.

The following Monday, the atmosphere amongst the band members was mixed at the field. There were more parents than normal in attendance, and while I'm sure a few of them wanted to see if Taylor was still capable of running the band, others just wanted to be there to support his efforts. The town, and the school for that matter, had never seen anything like what Taylor had put together over the last year.

Taylor used a bullhorn to assemble the members, and while that was standard operating procedure, it was a good thing, because Taylor's voice was beginning to weaken measurably as he was becoming short of breath.

After two run-throughs of their routine, Taylor looked over and saw Jamaal walking towards him and Mr. Harmon.

"Well, would you look at that," he said to Mr. Harmon. Bob wasn't aware of the story behind the two.

"So, you decided to give it a go, huh?" he shouted over to the young man as he approached.

"Maybe."

"I figured you'd show up."

"Well, I figured that if you could do it, show up I mean, then I can do it better."

"Oh really?"

"Yeah. I thought I'd try it for a little bit."

"A little bit? Jamaal, if you want to do it right, it's for the entire season, and believe me, it will require a lot of time and energy. It will also take discipline. That's the way it is with anything you'll do that's worthwhile in life. If you're going to do it better than me, you're going to have to be in it for the long haul. I know I am." The two just stared at each other for a moment.

"Yeah, okay, what the hell? I don't have anything going on this summer anyway. Where do I stand?"

"For what?"

"For the band, what do you think I mean?"

"Who said you were in the band? I think if you want to be where these people are, you're going to have to pay the price. They have. They've been out here all summer sweating away while you've been home loafing around. I think you owe them at least an audition."

"An audition? Are you crazy? I can run circles around anyone here...and you too. I've heard you play."

"Well then this should be a piece of cake for you, don't you think?" There was a pause. "If you want in, you're going to have to earn your way in. How about it? Right here, right in front of everyone."

"Go to hell. I don't need this." Jamaal turned to walk away.

"Fine, be a loser then." Taylor turned his attention to the assembled masses. Through the bullhorn, he yelled, "Okay everyone, let's take it from the top. Once more, with a little more zip."

"Hey!" Jamaal yelled. A couple of instruments in the band went off before a few of the band members realized that this discussion wasn't over. Jamaal stood there for a spell, feeling humiliated that he had to stoop to the level of a novice. "What the hell do you want me to do?"

Taylor smiled. "First and foremost, I want you to clean up your language a bit. Next, let's see what you can do. Dazzle us. You must have an extensive repertoire of rolls, beats, and sounds that have never graced our ears. Donny, give him your set for a minute."

Donny lifted his snare assembly off his shoulders and handed it to Jamaal. "The stage is all yours."

Jamaal looked at Taylor with scorn, but he didn't back down, and he didn't disappoint. He secured the snare in place, then preceded to make that drum sing. In between measures, he took the time to spin the sticks around his fingers, one at a time, showing everyone that he was not only good, but also nimble. He finished off by marching towards Taylor, then slammed both sticks on the snare in Taylor's face three times. Shouts of approval came from the assembled masses. He was good. Actually, he was better than good.

Taylor stood up, put his arm around Jamaal's shoulders, and turned their backs towards the band. In a quiet voice he said, "You're much too talented to beat on a bucket and beg for dollars for the rest of your life, son. You understand the chemistry, the make-up of music. Don't waste that. You also have the potential to teach some of these newbies what it takes, because you know. You've been there. You're incredibly talented. Use that to your advantage."

Taylor turned the two of them back towards the band, then he raised his voice and proclaimed, "As for this summer, your card is now full. Welcome to the band." The assembled masses cheered.

The first game of the season was now less than a month away, but still the inevitable occurred. Taylor only made it to two practices the following week because he just wasn't feeling up to it. It was apparent that he was becoming weaker by the day. His doctor told him to expect that. I'm sure his illness was progressing at a rapid rate due to the fact that he had refused most of the traditional chemotherapy. Early on, he wasn't too eager to continue on in life. Yes, he now took his meds, and while they were helpful, it only arrested the symptoms for so long. Since this disease was incurable, he asked, "What was the use?"

Kaylee still had the flag corps to deal with, so she had a responsibility to show up at the field daily. When Taylor couldn't make it to practice, I would go over to his place on those days and keep him company. He was generally in good spirits, and we passed the time talking over old times. We talked over our childhoods, our neighborhood friends, and our families. You know, up until then, Taylor and I never really sat down and talked as adults about…things, you know? I guess sometimes we can become so busy with the events of everyday life that we forget to actually live.

Until he told me after he returned to town, I never realized that Taylor's father had been a hardcore alcoholic or that his mother had been as loose in her morals as she was. Oh, I had my suspicions, of course, and people did talk, but as the old song goes, no one knows what goes on behind closed doors. It's true.

Since Taylor had moved away at an early age, his recollection of those we used to hang around with ended back in the year 1967. I had to fill him in on all of the 'whatever became of's.'

"Tammy Stevens, remember her? She ended up running away the day after graduation. I think her uncle who lived with them was molesting her, or so I've been told. It's sad, but no one really knows whatever happened to her, even today."

"Wow, and I had such a crush on her."

"Everyone did. She had a chest on her, now; a real head turner, that girl."

"That she did. Wasn't she the one who always wanted to play center when we got a touch football game up?"

"One in the same."

"That's too bad. I wish we had known."

"Oh, remember Bill Simpkins?"

"Wimpy Simpy? Lived down near the corner? Hell yes. He sure earned that nickname. He couldn't hit a ball with a bat if you paid him. Don't tell me he went on to play major league baseball."

"Oh no," I said with a laugh. "In fact, it turns out he was gay."

"No way. Aw, and I think of all of the names we used to call him and how we'd make fun of him. I guess we should have thought before we spoke. We never know how much we might be hurting someone."

"True, but you have to remember, we didn't know. Hell, we were being kids, and that's what kids do. They can be so mean."

"I have so many regrets in life, Smitty. That is one of them."

"We all do. So long as we learn from our mistakes, I suppose."

Much of our time together was spent in spiritual introspection. It was an enlightening experience for both of us. Now mind you, Taylor wasn't the perfect patient. He at times complained about his lot in life. Not all of it, just the agonizing times he would have wanted to avoid, given his druthers. I did my best to try and keep him honest.

"So, what would you change, given the chance?"

"Oh, I'm sure much of my life would remain as it was, but the painful times, man, they really took their toll on me."

"Yes, but it was the mix of your good and bad times together that made up the quilt of your soul. Isn't that how you referred to it, the quilt of your soul? Let me ask you, did you ever think that when you started out in life you'd become a rock star?"

"No, I don't suppose so. That would have been too wild."

"And yet, it was the trouble you had with your teachers, as well as your parents, that shoved you into the world of entertainment. Am I right?"

With some hesitation, Taylor answered, "Well, yes, in a round-about way." He was thinking over that revelation, and beginning to realize that life indeed wasn't his enemy.

"You see, if you had dodged all of the bad in your life, you might have spoiled the surprise."

"Yeah, surprise." Taylor just smiled.

On an off day the following week, Taylor asked me if I'd take him to the cemetery. I told him I would gladly give him a lift. We drove over, and I had to help him out of the car and into a wheelchair. He didn't need one all of the time, like around the house, but if he was going to take more than a few steps, the chair was a safe bet.

I stayed back at the car while Taylor wheeled over to his parents' graves. I felt for him because he was anything but comfortable in a wheelchair, but he knew he had little in the way of options at this point of his illness. He just became too winded while on his feet.

On this outing he did okay, but while rolling across the grass, his wheel got hung up on a pine cone. Taylor charged at it once or twice in an attempt to clear the obstacle, but failed each time. I wanted to go over and help him, but before I left the car, he finally gave up and went around it. He rolled up in front of the twin markers, stared quietly for a moment, then had his say.

"You know, there was a time I hated you both because of the chains you saddled me with in this life. But I guess like they say, sometimes we never even know we have the key. Be that as it may, we all have to play the parts assigned to us in this drama we call life. They might not be the roles we tried out for, and we might not end up sporting the grandest robe, but the only person we have to be better than is ourselves. As a result, the pieces of life's puzzle fall into place and begin to reveal the final picture as our time here on this plane nears a completion. As difficult as it is for me to say, I have to say thank you for at least giving me the opportunity to prove myself and do what I can for my fellow man here in this world. I guess it can truly be said about me and my life, better late than never. I became all that I could become. At least I wanted you to know that I now understand." Taylor just looked at the stones for a moment, then said, "See you soon."

I helped Taylor back into the car and he asked me to drive up him up to the main office. I did, but I felt rather strange in doing so. I knew what he was going to do, and I have to say in all honesty that I've never been with anyone who shopped for a grave plot, knowing full well that they would occupy it sooner rather than later.

We entered the office, and they asked if they could help us.

"Yes, my parents are buried in section X, and I wanted to know if I could purchase the plot next to them."

The salesman pulled out the map and had Taylor point out the approximate location of the Taylors. He told us that being an older section, the only open plot was next to Mrs. Taylor, but it had already been purchased.

221

"By whom? Perhaps I can offer to buy it from them."

"It's already owned by, well as it is, it's owned by Leonard Taylor. Isn't that your father?"

"Yes. How do I, or can I, get it transferred into my name?"

"Well, let me see. Okay, here we are. He lists it as going to the next of kin within the Taylor family in the paperwork on file here. Upon his demise, the plot is automatically transferred to you. I take it you're the sole survivor of the Taylor clan?"

"Yes sir, that's me."

"Well then, all I'll need to see is proper identification, and we can get the paperwork under way."

There was a problem, but only a minor one, concerning the transfer. You see, Taylor Ross was no longer a 'Taylor.' He was now legally a 'Ross,' so he had to produce the correct papers to prove that he really was a relative of the current owners.

The first game of the season was just a week away, and Taylor unexpectedly took a turn for the worse. I knew he had been pushing it. I could see the stress on his face every time he tried to get up. He eventually had to be hospitalized with respiratory problems, and we all feared that he wouldn't make it to see the culmination of his efforts. If so, it would have been a perfectly sad ending to an otherwise remarkable life.

Taylor did stabilize and was released on Wednesday, two days before Hamilton took on North Haverbrook, and the Big Blue band unveiled its new look. At this point, he was considerably weaker and was given supplemental oxygen to use when he felt the need.

As desperate as the situation looked for all of us involved, everything was actually right on schedule. It's funny how life does that. Just when you think the wheels are about to fall off the cart, you meet a man with a wrench. That's what happened with Taylor's situation. No, he didn't need a wrench to fix the wheel on his chair, but he did need a pick-me-up. You see, the biggest moment in his life was about to occur, and a bout of depression was overtaking him.

Once he was released from the hospital, he knew his days out of a wheelchair were all but over and a sense of finality began to take over. He just didn't have the strength to get up and move around on his own anymore. He could pull himself out of his chair and into a more comfortable chair, or into a bed for that matter, but for all practical purposes, his walking days had come to an end.

Taylor wasn't the only one saddened by this sudden turn of events. I was on the outside, but when Taylor became chair-ridden, I could feel him beginning to slip away. No, he hadn't given up on life, but it almost seemed as if a part of his spirit had already begun the first part of its final journey.

Now, I have to say, despite keeping a low profile, Kaylee was still a major force in Taylor's life. Not only was she busy helping Mr. Harmon with the band and keeping her flag carriers in step, she had been working on a special project for several weeks now. She hoped to have it complete before Friday night's game. Never tell Kaylee that something can't be done, because she'll find a way to bring it to fruition.

A couple of weeks before, Kaylee contacted Taylor's agent, Jerry Langdon, and asked him to check into the guitarist who had played with Taylor on the Letterman show a year ago. Jerry not only got her a name, but also gave her the man's phone number. She called Justin Neumann and explained to him who she was and what her situation was in Ohio. He was understandably shaken, but he did verify that he was indeed Taylor's son.

Apparently, Justin's mother left Taylor once she found out she was pregnant, and she had every intention of fleeing to Mexico, getting a divorce, then an abortion, then getting on with her life. She got the quickie divorce, but kept the child. She raised Justin on her own, mostly, but didn't tell him of his birth father's background until he was in high school and was excelling musically. Anyway, Justin readily agreed to drop everything and come to town to meet with Taylor.

Taylor had no clue of what was about to occur. Kaylee really didn't have time to notify him of the impending introduction because Justin's arrival was up in the air until the very last moment. She didn't want to get his hopes up just in case.

That Thursday, I stayed with Taylor while Kaylee went to the airport to pick up Justin. When he stepped into the terminal, Kaylee had no trouble spotting him. He was a handsome fellow; looked much like a younger, healthier version of Taylor. Justin had no trouble spotting Kaylee. She was the one crying while staring in his direction.

They embraced, then Kaylee called me on her cell phone and told me they were on their way. She left it up to me to prepare Taylor. That was fine. I decided to wait until the moment grew close to cut down on Taylor's anticipation.

On the way home, Kaylee filled Justin in on everything that had gone on during the last nine months or so. It took her nearly the entire one-hour trip home to complete the story, and during that time, Justin barely got a word in edgewise. Kaylee later apologized, but Justin appreciated her effort.

"Tay," I began, "I was talking to Kaylee the other day, and she said something about…well, this is going to be tough…but she mentioned that you ran into a fellow a year or so ago who claimed to be you son. His name was something like Justin and he was a guitarist."

Taylor just looked at me for a moment, trying to figure out how I had finagled that information out of Kaylee. Finally, he spoke up and said, "Yeah, something like that."

"Do you think he actually is your son?"

"Probably."

"His last name is Neumann, just like your ex-wife's maiden name, right?"

"Yes. How did you know that?"

"Taylor," I said as I wiped my face with my hand, "Kaylee located Justin and spoke with him."

"She did. What did he say?" He began looking around. "Where is she, anyway?"

"Tay, she's at the airport. She went to pick him up."

"He's coming here?"

"Yes, he wanted to see you, to speak with you."

"Here? Well, I don't look, I-I mean…"

"Tay, you're fine. Here let me get you a comb for your hair. Other than that-"

Just then, I noticed Kaylee pulling into the driveway.

"Okay, they're here. You look fine. Are you okay with all of this?"

"A little late to ask me that." I was worried, but after a moment, he smiled and replied, "Of course I'm okay with it. This is long overdue."

Now, before they arrived at the house, Kaylee did her best to advise Justin on what to expect from Taylor. Even in a week's time, his health had declined noticeably. Needless to say, he was a mere shadow of the man Justin had played next to on national television just a year ago.

They came up the walk and through the front door. Kaylee was beaming, and Justin followed behind looking a bit more tentative.

Justin was a good-looking man. Yes, he did remind me a little of Taylor, but he was a little heavier and certainly a bit more robust than his predecessor, but the Taylor look was there. He may have had an inch or so on the old man as well.

"Tay, I'm sure you remember Justin. Justin, meet your father…again, Taylor Ross."

"Hey Tay-or dad. I'm really not sure what to call you."

"Taylor is fine. I don't think I qualify to be called 'dad.'"

Justin set his bag down, walked over to shake Taylor's hand, and their greeting gravitated into a light embrace, then the two engaged in an all-out hug. The eyes of both men moistened up as they held each other. Taylor kept saying, "I'm sorry, I'm sorry I wasn't around."

Justin kept answering, "That's okay, man, it's okay."

226

Justin stayed the night, and he and Taylor caught up on each other's lives well into the wee hours. They finally called it a night and agreed to get some sleep, as the following day was one we had all been waiting for.

Chapter 7

**One Final Note**

*"...and in the end, the love you take*

*is equal to the love you make."*

~ Paul McCartney, The Beatles' *The End*

The night of the band's great unveiling, if you will, was a typical warm, late August evening. Nearing game time, the temperature was still in the lower eighties, and because of that, I worried about the effect it could have on Taylor's health. Being confined to a wheelchair and occasionally short of breath, he was rarely comfortable these days. Despite his Herculean effort with the band, Taylor wasn't sure that he wanted to attend that night's ceremony. I can only surmise it was because he felt he wouldn't be able to fully participate. Taylor didn't like to do anything 'half-assed,' as he put it. He was also very self-conscious about his current status as disabled person. He wasn't used to that either, but Justin talked him into it.

"I want to see you and your band, Pop," he said playfully.

The powers-that-be had been busy out at the field much of the day, setting up for the big night. There was so much to do. The school had never seen such a presentation. The carpentry class even rolled a large scissor jack down to the field for use as a temporary stage for Taylor to lead the band. I wasn't sure how well they could pull that off in his condition, but Bob Harmon, of all people, came up with an ingenious solution.

228

"Jason, bring me the air compressor." The band had a portable air tank on the sidelines that they planned to use with a boat whistle during a number at the halftime show.

"Bryan, can I borrow a roll of athletic tape for a moment?" he called over to the athletic trainer. Harmon took the white fabric tape and fastened the air hose to a whistle. Not only was that move ingenious, it showed that through it all, Bob Harmon hadn't lost his love for his fellow man, no matter what difficulties they may have gone through in the past.

We tried to get Taylor over to the field as early as possible, but even under the best of circumstances, those things can take time. We pulled up to the main entrance, and it was already packed with people coming and going into the field. Justin and I unloaded Taylor's chair, then helped him into it. We did our best.

People stopped and stared, some out of curiosity, some out of a sense of awe, for the hometown people knew of Taylor's plight. They also knew how much he had given back to the community.

The policeman opened the main gate, the same one the players run through as they enter the field, and we were able to wheel Taylor directly on to the track. When we guided Taylor into place facing the field from the east end zone, Kaylee leaned down and placed a kiss on Taylor's cheek. "You did good, hon."

Taylor looked to Kaylee. "I've never failed at anything I've set this mind to in this life. I feel," he said, while choking up, "that I'm failing the students now," he said between labored breaths, "because I'm bailing on them," he said in a near whisper.

"Hon, when we're thrust into this life, none of us has a choice in our fate. We just have to do the best we can with what we have. And as for failing, Taylor, you probably accomplished more in this past year than you have in your previous sixty."

He patted her hand that rested on her shoulder. "It's only fifty-five, dear. I only look sixty."

She smiled. It was good to see that he hadn't lost his sense of humor.

"And on top of that, you didn't fail. Taylor, the two girls who left the band when Mr. Harmon departed last fall, rejoined on Monday. You did it. The band is two hundred and eighty members strong."

"So, basically, Bob Harmon accomplished that goal."

"Now, don't start that. You did it. They came back because, like you said, everyone else was in the band, and they felt left out. You said that would happen. You created the groundswell. You accomplished your goal."

That got a smile out of him. "I believe you said that, dear, but I suppose I helped," he conceded.

I drove the van over to the practice field and parked it. On my way back to the gate, the Hamilton players were making their way from the locker room down to the field, chanting their war songs and clapping as they went. I tagged along, then yielded the gate to them as it was opened and they filed onto the track. As they did so, an interesting thing took place.

Throughout modern high school history, for the most part, unless the school was particularly small, there has been an unwritten rule that rarely do the band and athletic teams mix. Oh, there have been some music students who participated in athletics, and a few of the athletes who contributed during music classes, but generally speaking, the hard-core musical students had their cliques, and the athletic teams had their mates. To be fair, the two groups probably had more in common than they realized, but many times it still boiled down to a case of geeks versus jocks.

However, on this evening, as the chanting football team entered the track, they quieted themselves and slowed their jog to a walk. They did their best to form a single file line, then approached Taylor as he sat facing the field. As they passed by, each player gave words of encouragement to Taylor, patted him on the back, and thanked him for all he had done. With eighty players on the team, it took a while for them to pass, but it was worth the wait. Taylor was startled at first, but then he basked in the glow of satisfaction.

I stood there and watched until the trainers, equipment managers, and coaches passed by and bestowed their words of encouragement as well.

As I turned to enter the field, I heard the roar of the drums from the approaching Hamilton band as they marched from the school's band room and down the driveway on their way towards the field. I had a decision to make whether to go in now, or risk having a better viewing perspective from outside the gate. I wanted to see what the band looked like in all their glory–the finished product if you will–so I stayed put.

I have to admit that aside from staring in wonderment at this beautiful spectacle, I had to smile with great satisfaction. For you see, parked next to the fence was the equipment bus for the North Haverbrook Cardinal band, and painted along the vehicle's side in script, intertwined amongst a myriad of musical notes, was the slogan, 'Biggest Band in the Land.' They were a sizable ensemble to be sure, they always have been, but the members who were preparing to reclaim their instruments, stood to the side to allow the Big Blue marching band to pass by.

What a sight it was. Those band members passed and passed and passed. Why, there were so many blue and white clad members of that band passing by me that I began to wonder if they were marching in a complete circle in an attempt to appear as if they were many times larger than they actually were. It was no illusion, however, as 'the biggest band in the land' discovered that they might have to hire a sign painter to add the word 'second' to the slogan on their bus.

I followed the last member onto the track, and the gates were closed behind us. The packed house was cheering wildly as the band continued funneling onto the field. I walked over to Taylor. He just stared at the spectacle as the members of the band began to cover the playing surface. Several of the members glanced quickly over at Taylor, while others didn't have the courage to do so. They just stared straight ahead, but they knew Taylor was there.

"Now that's a band," Taylor said.

As it was nearly time for the performance to begin, I looked over and nodded to the fellows who had been waiting patiently over by the concession stand. Nobody paid any attention to these men, for they could have been any of the players' fathers, or grandfathers for that matter. To the average Joe, they were an undistinguished trio. Taylor would recognize them, however, and they had been very relevant to him during his life.

When Kaylee was talking to Taylor's agent about Justin, he was able to contact the remaining members of Vulture and tell them what we had planned. They all were in agreement that it was time to let bygones be bygones, and the stage was set for them to come to the forefront and stand up for their comrade.

232

Ernie Huber, Pete Dixon, and Joe Paxton walked over to where we were.

"If you were any more stoned, you'd be a rock, a Taylor Rock," stated Joe. Taylor knew that voice. He knew that statement as well, for he heard it from Joe's mouth many times during their playing years. Taylor turned and saw the three approaching.

"Oh my God; Pops, Red, C.J." was all he could mutter as he was overcome with emotion by the appearance of his old friends. His shaking hand covered his mouth in disbelief, for this was the last thing Taylor expected. He never thought he'd see his former band mates again in this lifetime, especially now. He thought it was over many years ago. The group's break-up hadn't been pretty; things were said, you know.

The three gathered around Taylor, rubbing his shoulders, patting his back, and then all four traded hugs. Taylor couldn't help but smile as big as I've ever seen him. Tears flowed freely from these graying, balding men who once embodied a 'screw everyone but yourself' attitude.

After they exchanged 'good to see you's,' Ernie said, "We've heard of all the good you've been doing lately, and we just had to see it for ourselves. We didn't think you had it in you! You're an old softy after all, you old S.O.B."

"Marvelous, marvelous," was all Pete could say as he clapped his hands while viewing all of the members of the marching band, a band that was now the size of many major college marching bands, as they filed into place.

The crowd was reaching its fever pitch, so Joe kneeled down and shouted to Taylor, "Remember when you played that gig with Jerry Lee Lewis in the early eighties and said that you came away from that session a changed man, because that was the pinnacle of your career? It was the real deal, you said, because he was the true spirit of Rock and Roll. Well, you changed a lot of people's lives here today and for some time to come, because this is the real deal. This is your mountaintop, Taylor. Despite your physical weakness, this is the time when your spirit is at its strongest, has climbed its highest, and will shine its brightest. Taylor, today you are a mensch," Joe said, harkening back to his nearly forgotten Jewish roots. He planted a light-hearted but enthusiastic kiss on Taylor's cheek. For him, it was the ultimate compliment.

Taylor patted Joe's hand and weakly said, "Thank you."

I hated to break up this special moment, but it was time for the ceremonies to begin. "Well, let's get this show on the road," I said.

The last few members of the marching band were claiming their spots on the field. If the situation hadn't been so bittersweet, the scene to follow would have been almost comical. It seemed as if everyone wanted to grab hold of Taylor's throne and help him over to the stage. Everyone wanted to touch the king's robe. All six or seven of us traveled as a pack.

We rolled the forty or so yards across the chunky rubberized track until we reached the mid-point of the field. We pushed Taylor's wheelchair onto the scissor jack's platform, then locked the wheels into place.

Taylor took a moment to look around at the members of the band, his band, and still most of them stared straight ahead...just like he had taught them. Third down the line of drummers was Jamaal. He glanced over for only a moment, then in an attempt to avoid crying, scrunched his face up and ended up looking a bit like famed trumpet player Louis Armstrong when he was in the process of gracing the airwaves with a high 'C'.

Taylor looked towards the stands and spotted Jamaal's mother, Frieda Payton, in the front row, crying. Taylor knew she wasn't shedding tears for him. Rather, she was overcome that her son had finally found a focus, and for the first time in his life, had stuck with something and had seen it through.

As Taylor was now in place, I looked around and asked, "Okay, now how do we operate this thing?"

Kaylee spoke up and said, "Hold on. We're not ready for that yet. Principal Dooley?"

Principal Charles Dooley, with the microphone in hand, walked up to Taylor. He thumped the mic once to see if it was on, and it was. The thump produced a squeal from the public address speakers mounted on the light standards. The feedback silenced just as rapidly as it began. Principal Dooley, now with furrowed brows, looked up to the press box to make sure the sound levels were correct, then he began.

"Taylor, we're all gathered here tonight not just to witness a fine athletic competition between these two first-rate schools, but we also would like to pay tribute to your exceptional effort. It was your challenge to the students of Hamilton High, and your example and inspiration that put this incredible band on the field tonight. For that we would like to express our gratitude to you."

There was a prolonged amount of cheering and applause.

"Words can only convey so much appreciation. We cannot repay you for all of the volunteer hours you put into this project, but we can do something for you. You had to leave Hamilton High before you were able to graduate, so it is my honor to present to you, a diploma signifying you as an honorary graduate of Hamilton High School. Bob."

Principal Dooley looked to Bob Harmon, who then walked over to Taylor with the diploma, opened it, and placed it in Taylor's lap. "Congratulations, *Ross*. You learned your lessons well and earned not only this degree," he said as his voice began to sharply crack, "but the respect of all here. Job well done, my friend." The crowd cheered on.

Taylor just stared at the diploma, then back at Mr. Harmon. With heavy eyes, Bob just pursed his lips and nodded at Taylor. Taylor looked once more at the certificate, and a tear fell from his eye and landed square on the diploma making the ink spelling out his name run a bit. I didn't want to see it get ruined, so I folded it over and freed it from his lap.

"Well, there's just one thing left to do, Tay. Time to get this show started."

Bob Harmon set the portable air tank on the lift, then handed the air hose to Taylor and explained, "I knew you probably wouldn't have the breath to sound the whistle to start the band, so I rigged this up. See, if you place this in the palm of your hand and squeeze, the air will release and the whistle will sound."

He handed the odd-looking contraption to Taylor. Taylor looked at it, positioned it in his hand and gave it a gentle squeeze. A small whistle sounded. That surprised Taylor and he let loose with an, "Oh!" He saw that with a good squeeze, the whistle would sound louder and sharper than he probably could have delivered as a healthy man. He placed the unit in his lap, looked at Mr. Harmon, then slowly reached into his shirt pocket and drew out a gold-plated whistle. It was the same gold whistle Mr. Harmon threw at Taylor's feet during the night of their spat. He handed it to Bob.

Mr. Harmon's hand shook as he took the keepsake he thought was long gone. You see, this was no ordinary whistle. This was given to Mr. Harmon by the High School Band Director's National Association in recognition of the half century he dedicated to directing marching bands and educating students in instrumental music. It was really meant for display and not for daily use, but Mr. Harmon was proud of it and liked to show it off. "If you can't use it, what good is it?" he once said. He clutched it to his chest.

"Oh my God, thank you, Taylor."

Taylor smiled, then said, "It's an honor. You earned it."

Principal Dooley asked, "Tay, are you ready to face your people?" Taylor nodded in the affirmative. Principal Dooley slowly began elevating the scissor jack upwards until it hit a ten foot height. I thought they were going to raise him only five or six feet, but Dooley gave him a full ten spot. I hoped it wasn't too high for Taylor, with him being in a wheelchair and all, but he didn't seem to mind. In fact, I think he was up high enough to overlook the entire band and see each and every member. He just stared right then left at the group.

The band covered the area between the goal lines of the football field where there were alternating lines of fourteen band members from sideline to sideline, followed by the next line holding thirteen musicians, give or take. It went that way until each half of the field held one hundred and forty members. Kaylee's twenty flag carriers anchored the end zone portions of the formation.

It must have been a sight to behold for Taylor. This was the climax of not only a year's worth of his finest work, but perhaps the culmination of his life's purpose. But the puzzle wasn't complete. Taylor hadn't been around the band in several weeks. He hadn't heard them in their polished, completed form yet.

Despite a standing room crowd of nearly five thousand, at this point one could practically hear a pin drop. Most realized that it was Taylor's swansong, and they respected that.

"Are you okay, Tay?" I shouted up. He had been there for more than a moment. I knew why, but still, it was time.

Taylor didn't look back. He just nodded his head slightly, then straightened up in his chair. The band sensed he was ready as well as they snapped their instruments into place. Taylor gripped the air nozzle, looked out over the field, then his whistle pierced the air with the one-two-one-two-three-four cadence to begin the school's song. What followed, despite my best efforts, can't be described adequately with the written word. You had to be there.

The explosion from the forty-eight drums echoed off the bleachers on the north side of the field, then thundered back from the brick siding of the apartment buildings to the south. What began as a segmented drum roll, almost identical to the fanfare heard at the beginning of many Twentieth Century Fox movies of the past, was followed by the brass being raised and blasting their short piece to the heavens. As it was written, the first several stanzas of the song becomes somewhat of a battle between the percussion and horn sections as they echo each other's part. When the horns take the repeating measure up an octave, the drums answer back harder and louder. The entire band then joins in for the body of the song. That's when the marching begins.

The Hamilton High Fight Song was arranged by, ironically enough, Irvin C. Hamilton, no relation, back in the day when marches were popular, and Sousa would have been proud.

The band began marching towards the east end zone, with the first line curling back towards the opposite goal line. They were marching in a 'U' shaped formation, much the same way that the

Texas Longhorn Band performs their wall-to-wall march. I'm not sure how much of the song the people in the stands heard as they were all on their feet cheering the entire time. Even those sporting the crimson, white, and blue from North Haverbrook stood out of respect. It was truly a spectacle. Any college band would be proud to give such a performance.

I glanced up at Taylor and his eyes were glued to the scene before us. It appeared as if he was lost in the sight and sound, as well as a feeling of oneness with the music, a oneness with the community. His hand was moving slightly, almost automatically, as if trying to set the tempo. I saw a gleam in Taylor's eye that I hadn't seen since he performed live for the first time in high school. It was a sense of satisfaction. It was a sense of accomplishment. The spectacle of that evening echoes in my mind and heart still to this day.

Thinking back, the ending to this saga was bittersweet. You see, Taylor never did see the band perform again after that first game of the season. He also never got the chance to say good-bye to many of those who went the extra mile for the band, and the school. I'm sure Taylor's pride was part of the reason. He said that he was embarrassed to be seen at less than one hundred percent. Unfortunately, he predictably got worse as the days drifted by during that fall of 2005. And when he did stabilize, he just felt out of it for the most part. He thought that those who had sacrificed so much, deserved better than half a body and half a mind in a wheelchair. He was awfully hard on himself. They deserved the best, he said. I'm sure the band members would have gladly accepted anything he could give. They always did.

Anyway, after the opening game's conclusion, we all gathered back at my place. The rest of the night was spent in fellowship and celebration. It was quite an evening to be sure. Despite the late hour, for old time's sake I fired the grill up, tossed on a few burgers, and topped it off with Taylor's favorite dish–corn on the cob. He wasn't able to handle it the way he wanted, of course, but Kaylee helped him and he was ever so grateful.

After the meal, we settled down in the living room and talked, joked, and sang into the wee hours of the morning. The neighbors didn't complain, and to be honest, I think they knew our situation.

We were mightily impressed as Justin picked up a guitar and joined with the surviving members of Vulture to play some of their classics. Justin played John's part on his guitar, and he proved to be very skillful. His voice even sounded a bit like Taylor's. I guess talent does run in families.

The evening finished up just like one of the old jam sessions that Taylor and the boys used to hold back in the days of Haight-Ashbury. Taylor added his two-cents' worth as he thumped his hands on the arms of the chair keeping time with each song, and he managed to join in on every other word. His physical ability was nearly gone, but the songs were still in his heart.

They ran through several takes of a new song, their last song, Taylor had written just a month earlier, titled *Taking Flight*. In its initial run-through, the song almost took on a dirge-like quality. But, the group sparked it up a bit, and by the time the night was concluding they had an upbeat, kicky little tune on their hands.

The wind kissed our wings when the king donned his cape,

And so to the bay we made our escape.

And that was a feat, you know?

240

For we had never done a show,

In the town called San Francisco.


So we sang, we laughed; it came from our hearts,

We smoked we joked, then we topped the charts,

Asked what kind of beasts were we?

We were birds that now were free,

Free birds, would you remember me, I say,

Would you remember me?


We chewed and clawed and fed off the crowd,

Our style of playing was unquestionably loud,

And yet our notes have been swept away,

On the ears of yesterday,

And our time is now day to day.


We flew towards our dream but we ran out of sky,

That's when our orders came down from the guy,

So, until it was time to depart,

We knew right in our heart,

We would never be apart. Oh no,

We would never be apart.


That was an evening to remember. It was also one of the last times Taylor ever felt well enough to participate in anything so strenuous. Despite that, he rarely complained. The only time Taylor showed any regrets over his situation was a day when he wasn't feeling very well, and I walked in to greet him. He said, "Well, well, you came to see what a dying man looks like."

"No," I answered, "I came to see my best friend."

A few of the band members did stop by the house on occasion, and Taylor put his best foot forward, but it was a struggle. He didn't fool anyone. They all knew he wasn't long for this world, but they wanted to see him anyway. He wanted to see them as well, but under his conditions. That just wasn't possible anymore. It really took quite a bit out of him.

There was one time, however, when Jamaal called, and surprisingly Taylor agreed to meet with him. Under the current conditions, that was unusual, but Taylor had spent so much time trying to get Jamaal to open up and find his true potential. He wasn't about to give up now. Despite how he felt, I think Taylor wanted to see what made Jamaal tick. I think he also wanted to see what made him so defensive.

It was around the first of October, a misty, wet day as I recall, when Jamaal stopped by. It was a Saturday afternoon. Jamaal knocked on the door and Kaylee let him in. She knew why he was there, and he, of course, knew his purpose, so few words were needed. Jamaal was well aware of Taylor's condition, but wasn't quite sure what to expect. This was new ground for the young man.

We got Taylor dressed that day, and we were fortunate that this was one of his more energetic periods. He was looking forward to his meeting with Jamaal, but he didn't want the young man to see him "all laid up," as he put it. "He'll see me all laid out soon enough," he said, expressing his angered sense of humor.

Taylor usually lounged around in sweats, so to dress up today made him feel special. He felt as if he was rejoining the human race, if for only a little while. With my assistance, Taylor carefully slipped into a comfortable chair, then took a bit to get settled into a satisfying position.

"How do I look?" he said with his arms spread a bit.

"Pretty darn good," I replied.

"Almost life-like, huh?"

"Hey, no feeling sorry for yourself."

Just then, Jamaal walked in guardedly.

"Um, Mr. Ross?"

"Hey, hey, hey! None of this 'Mr. Ross' crap. Whatever happened to 'hey man?'"

We all laughed. Jamaal sensed that he could open up to Taylor and realized that he wouldn't break.

"I'm sorry. It's just that I didn't want to, you know…"

"Jamaal, I'm sick. That's it in a nut shell. That's how I feel right now; I just feel a little bit sick. I don't feel like I'm dying. In fact, I don't know how that feels, so let's just leave it at that." Having gotten that out of the way, Taylor changed the tempo. "So, how are you doing? You look good. It's all of that marching I'll bet."

"Yeah, maybe."

"Okay fellows, we'll leave you two to talk. Either of you two want something to drink?" Kaylee asked.

"No, we're fine," both answered in uneven unison.

I followed Kaylee out of the room and closed the bi-fold doors behind us.

"How are you doing, man, for real, I mean."

"Eh," Taylor began. "Not great. I have my good days and my bad. My problem is a lack of energy. I guess that's how this disease slowly kills you. Your spirit is nothing but raw energy, you know, and the body contains that force and gives it a purpose. That's how life works. Once that energy begins to slip away, you're like a punctured balloon and you slowly deflate until you can no longer serve your purpose. I guess you can say that I've sprung a leak, spiritually speaking."

"That makes sense."

"So what brings you here, Jamaal?"

Jamaal takes a moment, begins to say something, then buries his head in his hands and begins to break down.

"Hey, hey, there will be none of that. This ain't no funeral."

Jamaal continues on for a moment, wipes his eyes on his sleeve, then clears his throat. He looked up, but wasn't actually staring at Taylor. He couldn't, not right now.

"I just wanted to say thank-you for all you've done for me. You know, after our first game, my mom actually said that she was proud of me. Proud of me!" he exclaimed with a raised voice while thumping his opened palm against his breast bone. "I mean, she's always been proud of us I guess, but she's never really said so, you know?"

"Jamaal, I didn't do anything for you. You did it. Give credit where credit's due."

"Tay man, no one's ever taken the time to try and help me out and actually cared whether I succeeded or failed like you did. It wasn't what you said but how you said it."

"I saw so much potential in you, Jamaal. I was hoping that your common sense would kick in and you would come to your senses. You did, and that's a credit to you and your upbringing. Did your parents teach you that?"

"My mom tries, but she can only do so much what with three of us, and my dad died five years ago."

"Oh, I'm-I'm sorry to hear that. What happened, cancer, a heart attack?"

"A drunk driver."

"Oh wow, I'm, sorry to hear that. Did they ever catch the guy?"

"He was the guy. He was drunk and hit a bridge abutment on an overpass."

"Damn Jamaal, I'm so sorry."

"I remember my dad best when I was little. He was a great guy then. Most of his friends didn't spend any time with their kids. Most of them didn't even stick around, but Dad did. He loved Mom; he loved us."

Jamaal got up to walk around the room while he spoke. He wandered over to a shelf containing some bric-a-brac, and checked them out while continuing.

"I remember when I was five, Dad went to the carry-out just down the block from us and bought me one of those little waffle ball and bat sets. He would pitch them to me for hours, but I couldn't hit a lick."

The two men laughed.

"He always told me that if I stuck with it, I would grow up to be another Ken Griffey Jr. I didn't, of course. About the time I would have become eligible for little league, Dad lost his job at the old GM plant when it closed its doors. That's when he began to drink."

"The GM plant, huh? That's where my dad worked. And like you, I too had to endure the drunken ramblings of my dad. Not a great way to grow up, is it?"

"No, not really. After that, I didn't see him too much. When I did, he was usually a mess, and I choose not to remember him like that."

The two just stared at the ground for a while, perhaps spiritually visiting that painful place one last time.

"Anyway, he was unemployed for some time. He worked part-time jobs here and there. He worked some construction when his back would allow. Anyway, he had been out of work for a spell when he decided to get away from us all and go out for a ride one night. He couldn't stand to face us when he didn't have a job, and it was getting to the point where we didn't really want him around.

That night he pulled his bottle out from under the car seat and drank and drove from one end of the county to the other. His pain finally ended for him that night as it transferred from his soul to ours. He was there for me when I was a little guy, but I wasn't there for him when he died. I still feel so guilty about that."

"I wasn't there when my dad died either, and to this day I really don't know how or when he actually passed away, but I don't feel any guilt about that. Perhaps I should. You know, both of our dads were angry men at the hand life had dealt them, and they took it out on themselves and, in the process, hurt those around them. I guess you and I are quite similar in many ways, Jamaal, but for different reasons. We can't allow our negative circumstances in life to turn us into the angry men our fathers became."

Jamaal stood silent for a moment. "You could be right. You challenged me to stick it out, the band that is, for the entire season, and I will. But I now challenge you to stick it out for the entire season. I don't want *you* to give up on you. You still have good to do in this world."

"Well, I've done my bit. How could I help anyone at this point being flat on my ass?"

Jamaal walked back over and sat in the chair across from Taylor. "You're helping me right now, aren't you?"

Taylor thought for a moment and tried to take in all he had just been told. Jamaal usually didn't say a lot, but when he did speak, it usually had far-reaching consequences.

"Jamaal, I-I don't, that is, your challenge might be out of my control, but I'll tell you what, if you can do it, I will too. Shake."

The two shook on it.

Taylor held Jamaal's hand for a spell. It almost seemed as if Taylor wanted somehow to pass his life-long talent on to a new generation through some sort of spiritual osmosis, and in return regain some of the youth and vigor that had left him.

Taylor stared at Jamaal's hand. "Son, I'll level with you; you're probably not going to be the next Ken Griffey Jr. But, these are very gifted hands, gifted in their own way. I would give anything to see where they will take you over the next fifty years. Don't waste that talent. Find your own voice."

"Tay, I'm so lost. How do I do that, find my own voice, as you put it?"

"Well, just don't be afraid to try new things. Eventually you'll stumble upon something that really grabs you. If you decide to build on it, and in doing so you realize that it's more of a joy than work, you'll know you're on to something great."

"I see."

"You have a choice to make here. You have a choice whether to be true to yourself and become what you're destined to be, or you can choose to become one with the masses. You can stand out, or you can blend into the background. What I'm saying is, you can set the trends, or you can follow them. It's up to you."

"I think I already stand out," he said followed by a small laugh. "I guess I'll just have to search for that voice you spoke of."

"Let me tell a story. Back when we formed Vulture, we were all just a bunch of street musicians playing the same song. We were nothing great. We called ourselves a band, but we really weren't, not in the true sense of the word. It didn't take us long to jell as a unit, however, and that showed us that we had something special. Some bands can play together forever, and never play as one, you know?"

"Sure."

"Anyway, we put together our first cover tune, *Goin' Home* by the Stones. It was such a damn long song, a bit too bluesy for my taste, but Pete did it so well, and the rest of us really got into it. Well, we had found our voice, and it really shocked us, at least me, to hear us all come together, jamming as we were, and hearing Pete's voice filling in the vocals. "So that's how we're going to sound, huh?" we said. It was an incredible revelation. We sounded pretty good, we liked it, so we knew we were on our way."

"That's great, Tay. I won't let you down."

"Don't let *yourself* down."

"I know you're right, and I know I can't get there overnight, but even now I find myself asking which direction I should follow or why I should stick around with the band today. I mean, they're okay and all, and it's been a great experience, but how much can I learn from them? In many ways, I'm so far ahead of most of them," he said with a shake of his head. "I want to get better and move up, but I can't if I stay in one place, you know?"

"Jamaal, you're looking at this too one-sided." Taylor stopped, then reached over the chair and picked up his oxygen mask. He held it to his face and took a draw. Jamaal was a little taken aback. Taylor continued. "Take this opportunity to learn how to interact with others. This is a great time for you to discover something about yourself. I can't argue with you; in many ways you are more musically gifted than some of the other members. So my advice to you is to use this time to teach them what you know. Share your musical gift not only with the fans in the stands, but also with the other students in the band. In doing so, you will learn not what's in a book, but what's in your head and what's in your heart. Help those less fortunate than you. Help them to become better musicians, and by doing so, you will become a better person."

The two sat there for a moment.

"This is a teaching moment for you in your life, yes, but also a learning time as well. In your case, Jamaal, they're one in the same." Taylor grinned, for he had had an epiphany. "Wow, I thought I was at a dead end just a moment ago, and yet here I am helping you. The lesson I taught you was almost identical to the one you taught me." They both stared at each other, and knew they were both right and needed to listen to one another.

"I can't argue with you then," Jamaal began. "I guess I do have a lot. I never thought of it in those terms. We don't have much at home, and I always thought of myself as being poor, but I suppose it's all in how you look at it, isn't it?"

Taylor shook his head. "Yes it is. Plus, I think you, like many people, judge a person's worth in terms of the money or possessions they've accumulated. There are other forms of wealth in this life, and since that's the case, you are truly gifted."

"Wow, teach you say. I don't know if I can pull something like that off."

"Jamaal, you'll never know unless you try, and I mean really try. Let me tell you something," Taylor said as he shifted a bit to get more comfortable. "I'm sure you've heard of Lucy on TV, you know, from the old I Love Lucy TV show? She will always be known as one of the all-time greats, but back when she was a young woman in drama class, they told her to find a new field of study. They said she was wasting her time trying to act because she was too shy. Can you imagine that; too shy. Maybe she was at that point in time, but look what she did when she really tried." The two laughed.

"I'm sure you're familiar with Michael Jordan aren't you?"

"Hell yeah."

"Of course you are. He might be the greatest of all time. Did you know he was cut from his high school basketball team? Look what he went on to do. He rewrote the NBA record books. Why? Because he tried even harder and never gave up. And finally, we all know Walt Disney; you know, Disneyland, the movies, Mickey Mouse, and all of that. Did you know he was let go from a newspaper one time because they said he had no original ideas? Same deal. I've said it before that if you don't sell out for your cause, what's the point? If you don't try, you'll never know your potential, and therefore you'll never know what it's like to truly live life to its fullest. Jamaal, never give up and never stop learning."

"Wow, if I do what you say, then I'll be okay?"

"Well," Taylor said as he scratched his head, "you'll be better off than if you didn't."

Jamaal looked at Taylor as if he has just been sold a bill of goods without a warranty. Taylor sensed that.

"Look Jamaal, there are no guarantees in life, but I'll tell you three things I have learned over my many years: Number one, there's more to life than luck, but not a lot more. Number two, what comes around doesn't always go around. And finally, sometimes the grass *is* greener on the other side of the fence."

Jamaal didn't say a thing. He was trying to file away all of Taylor's wisdom for future use.

"I know that might paint a bleak picture of what you will be up against for the next five or so decades, and I don't know if your dad was able to communicate that to you before he passed, but those are the facts of life. Life is not fair, despite what you may have heard. Sometimes when one door closes, you're just left in the dark. If you're lucky like me, you'll find someone special in your life to help light the way. But I'm telling you right here and now that common sense is the most important trait one can develop as an individual. Don't sit around expecting miracles; create them."

Taylor once again reset himself in his chair. "I'll tell you what, in my time I've met a number of people who were book smart, but they weren't able to interact very well with others. They didn't fare very well in life. Then there are others who were people smart thanks to time and experience, but they didn't have a lick of common sense."

Jamaal didn't take his eyes off of Taylor. He knew that, particularly at this time of his life, these bits of wisdom were most useful and priceless.

"I'll leave you with one last tidbit," Taylor continued. "Good doesn't always triumph over evil. People like to think it does, and that's nice for the story books and movies, but this is the real world, and things don't always turn out the way you'd like them to. Trust your best judgment and go by what you feel to be right, then let the chips fall where they may. Learn to balance the feelings in your heart with the wisdom in your head. President Reagan used to say, "Trust, but verify." I like that. When you master that approach, you will be the ruler over your destiny."

Jamaal and Taylor ended their meeting as they both needed time to digest the food for thoughts they took in that afternoon. Taylor was so drained afterwards that he reclined in that chair for the next three to four hours, sound asleep.

I sat with Taylor nearly every day during his last month. I usually did most of the talking, as Taylor wasn't very animated, either physically or emotionally, during that time. Sometimes he would just sit there, looking fine, but not feeling well enough to carry on a conversation. When we did talk, we would reminisce about the old days, how far we've come and all, and when I would hit the right nerve, we would laugh. Oh, how we would laugh! That was great therapy for Taylor, but it did my heart a lot of good as well.

We talked about a little bit of everything during those days. We talked about our loves and loves lost. Sometimes we would pass the time by just sitting in his bedroom and watching cartoons. He still loved watching *Tom and Jerry*. They were the 'Cadillac of cartoons,' as he put it. That was how we often passed the time when we growing up, except now fewer hours lay ahead of us than behind us.

Taylor grew very introspective as his time grew short. I'm sure that isn't unusual for a man in his situation.

"It really doesn't seem that long, my life. I mean, I guess I was so busy doing things that I lost track of time," he once said. "I almost feel as if I fell asleep one day while in high school, then woke up right back where I started, only many years later. The only difference is that I'm a whole lot older, and hopefully a little wiser. I suppose I missed a lot." I don't think he missed as much as he thought he did.

Needless to say, Taylor and Kaylee said their good-byes. It was a long good-bye, for when they both said 'I do' on the altar of matrimony, they knew their union would be brief. As such, each day began and ended with a greeting and a farewell from each of them knowing full well that one day soon only the former would be fitting.

Theirs was a private farewell, a day-by-day situation that I was not privy to. They chose to do it in this fashion because neither wanted a messy death bed scene that would turn a most difficult emotional situation, even more so.

Recognizing that his days were growing short, Taylor declared that he still wasn't ready to go yet. He said that so many things in his life were still incomplete. I was puzzled at that statement because I saw things quite the opposite in regards to his life. I ran down the schedule of his life and times, and how, in reality, everything was indeed complete. His unpleasant situation with his family pushed him in the direction that led to great personal fulfillment and professional success. After his time with Vulture had run its course, Taylor was given time off to be introspective with himself. That led him to the third stage in his life where he was to return home and put into practice the lessons he learned over his entire lifetime.

"You're complete, Taylor, more complete as a spirit than most of us will ever come to realize. Perhaps you weren't put here to march with the band out on the field. That's not your gig. You were brought back here to bring the young people of this town together and to show them that there's hope, there's a future, and their future is what they will make of it. It's in their hands, you told them. There doesn't have to be all of the glitz and glamour of Hollywood for one to be a success. You had that, and it was impressive to be sure, but your greatest accomplishment in life didn't occur on a world stage in front of millions of people, but from the time you spent in a little Midwestern town of sixty thousand." Taylor nodded his head in the affirmative.

Once when he was deep in thought, Taylor spoke of his ultimate demise. Despite being in control of much of his life, or so he thought, Taylor had trouble dealing with situations where he had little say.

"You know, I never really thought about an ending to my story. I always just thought I would go on forever." I saw a tear spill from the corner of his eye. "It wasn't supposed to end this way, you know. I was supposed to live until my spiritual light grew dim and my body was drawn up due to the weight of time. The story was supposed to get old to the point where no one wanted to read it anymore, and by the same token, no one wanted to write it anymore. Then, it would be time for life and me to part company."

Like it or not, that's exactly what was happening to him right now, but he couldn't see it. And even though people weren't 'tired of reading his story,' as he put it, it was still too soon for Taylor's taste.

"Yeah, I guess I've had it tough," he continued, "but we all have our challenges in life. You faced going to war, and yet you made it through in one piece. You're now facing a life alone, but you're making do." Taylor looked down. "My life seems so short, but in looking back, I guess so much has gone on in my fifty-plus years. We witnessed the rise of the rock revolution, what with The Beatles and all, and we were right up there with the leaders. We protested in the name of civil rights, and we were able to harvest the fruits of our labor. Now, I guess it's time for a rebirth in humanity, and I guess I was picked to be up front to lead that charge as well."

"You've been chosen, Taylor, because you're a born leader. You've always set the standard; you didn't follow the old rules. When life threw a roadblock in your path, it didn't stop you. You went around it, through it, or over it. You've always danced to your own tune, as they say, and now I guess it's time for you to embark on your greatest journey. You've passed life's courses with flying colors, and now your graduation day is approaching. No one will be happier than me to see you accept a diploma from the big guy himself, but it will also be a sad time, for parting is such sweet sorrow, as the old saying goes. I've grown to like the new Taylor Ross."

When his time was rapidly approaching, I knew it. So did Kaylee. A day or two before he passed, both of us spent the majority of our waking hours with Taylor. Through his mental haze, Taylor remarked to me on that first day that his mom visited him the previous night.

"It had been so long," he said with a weak voice. "She said that she wouldn't leave me this time. She left some white flowers over on the dresser. That was nice."

I looked over on the chest, and of course there were no flowers. I think that notion might have been flushed from his memory originating from a story he told me back when we were boys. I had nearly forgotten it. It was Easter morning, and Taylor saw some white flowers growing on the edge of a vacant lot in the neighborhood. He thought his mom would like them, so he put on his Easter service clothes and trudged through the weeds to get them. He returned only to have his mom scream at him for having soiled his good clothes. She sent him to clean the mud from his shoes as Sunday service was just an hour away, and I believe the flowers ended up in the garbage.

I knew that he was experiencing was what many refer to as having one foot in this life, and one in the next. That was so frightening to me because I knew he wasn't making that up. He truly saw and experienced those things, and knowing that would have to give anyone a pause and realize that something other than the concrete exists out there.

Later on, he would say little other than, "Smitty, I don't know...," and he would leave that sentence unfinished. He said that twice that I can recall. I think he wanted to say something along the line of, "Smitty, I don't know if I can pull this one out," but he was just too weak to finish.

After these last few visits with Taylor, I would go in the other room and break down. Kaylee would do her best to ease my pain, but she had plenty of her own to deal with.

It's been said that in life, you must learn how to live, and therefore you will know how to die. That way, you'll carry no burdens from this life into the next. Eventually, we all have to make peace with that which tortures and torments us.

Taylor did that, and despite getting lost in the sixties, he made up for those missing days with what little time he had remaining, proving that truly it's never too late to be who you were meant to be. He proudly chose his final place of rest next to his parents in section X out at Greenwood. Taylor's headstone simply read 'Ross Taylor.' I guess you could say that he took The Beatles' advice to just 'let it be.' Taylor returned to his roots shortly before he returned to the same Earth that gave him life. There was no reason to carry on the charade of a mega rock star with all of the money and fame anymore. It served its purpose.

But in a more profound sense, Taylor finally understood that one's time here on this plane is finite, so it's in one's best interest to make the most of it. No one is guaranteed seventy-plus years in this life. Taylor also came to realize that no matter how long the produce stands remained open, his will alone couldn't stop the seasons from changing. He didn't have the power to halt the inevitable. He made his peace with life in that respect too, then moved on.

The passing of a soul is never an easy transition. No one can imagine what's required of the individual in question when they pass over; we only know the difficulty for those of us left behind. Taylor said that when he was first diagnosed, he felt like he had been given a pink slip, a two-week notice, if you will, in life. He still had to show up for work while awaiting his final punch of the time clock, even though there was little to be gained in doing so. "It's all a part of falling apart," he would say.

I tried to comfort him the best that I could. "Don't worry guy, you won't be alone. I'll be along shortly. Just save me a seat on stage with you."

I've always had a tough time accepting the end of an individual's life. That's what hits me the hardest: the acknowledgement of my own mortality. I guess a lot of people go through that. Many feel that the passing of a loved one is the most difficult crisis they'll have to deal with in life. I'm sure that those more learned than myself would say that life has enough obstacles along the way, and if a friend's passing is the greatest tragedy that befalls an individual, then that person was very fortunate, or perhaps they just haven't lived life to its fullest.

It's sad actually, but to me, I look upon death as if the Almighty is writing a book about a life. He writes millions of them, you know. He always has. It seems the more he writes, the better he gets. Anyway, this living, breathing being is the main character, and God created that person's cast of significant others. But, when His hand tires and the pen is laid to the side, that life concludes, and the book is forever closed regardless of whether the main character has solved the crime, gotten the girl, or brought the particular situation to a satisfying conclusion. Many of us get no warning. While it's not the way we would do it on this plane, we eventually discover that we're not the author, but only a main character feeling our way through the pages of life.

The lead character in each story is afforded many avenues throughout each chapter, and yet they have to choose just one path for each life event. There is no right or wrong in this novel we call life. Things just are. In the end, those of us with our stories still ongoing are left with nothing but memories of our loved one's impressive tale, and how its ups and downs moved us in one direction or another. Upon their passing, we occasionally erect monuments, some physical, some spiritual, to enlighten later generations of this character's greatness, but in reality, when they're gone, they're truly gone. Society then looks to someone else to fill the void of this one-of-a-kind character.

I never thought I would get over my wife's passing a couple of years ago. She had been ill for some time, and one morning I needed to go out for some groceries. She told me not to worry and to go ahead. She would be here when I got back. I did, she was, but she wasn't, if you know what I mean. Life went on. I had no choice, but then neither did she.

It's been said that with each life, the die is cast early on, and we spend the rest of our days filling in that form with our life's deeds and accomplishments. In the end, we pop that mold, and what is, is for the entire world to see. But with Taylor, he danced to the beat of a different drum. He spent a lifetime constructing the mold, then he finally filled it in the blink of an eye. What emerged was just as it was supposed to be. He never did follow the rules, but his final achievement was just as beautiful as those who did; maybe more so, for everyone pulls for the underdog.

Taylor tried to put a positive spin on his passing, if that was possible. He said that he would have the last laugh in all of this. You see, without his living, breathing host from which to leech off of, his cancer was, in effect, committing suicide. And so it did.

On his deathbed, Taylor showed no apprehension about his fate. He had little concern as to whether he would end up playing a harp in heaven, or dodging pitchforks in hell. He was more concerned for Kaylee, Justin, myself, and of course, the members of the band. I guess our feelings of helplessness are mirrored by the dying. Their friends and way of life are leaving them as well.

When it was Taylor's time, I was bound and determined to see that his passing wouldn't be a lonesome one. I still felt guilty of leaving my wife in her time of need. We were all there, Justin, Kaylee, the supportive care nurse, and me. Justin sat on a chair in the corner and lightly strummed his guitar. Most of his songs were his own compositions, and it was very soothing. Occasionally he'd throw in a slow, acoustical version of a Vulture hit. I had to smile, for it reminded me of the first time I heard The Beatles' song *Helter Skelter* on Muzak in an elevator. The whole experience was a bit surreal to say the least, but I wouldn't have traded it for anything. God wouldn't have allowed it to happen any other way. Taylor could leave only like Taylor would leave this plane. He could do nothing else because he was Taylor. You see, it was part of His plan.

During his final hours, I tried to make things as easy as possible for Taylor, as I embraced him and told him that now his spirit was not unlike those kites we used to fly on Woodward Avenue many decades earlier. Now he'd earned the right to fly free, untethered, to discover other challenges and enjoy other experiences amongst the cosmos. He weakly agreed. "I guess my time is at hand," he said.

Taylor passed five days after the final football game of that 2005 season. It was a Wednesday. It was the best he could do. Come hell or high water, he wasn't going to allow the band's outdoor season to be overshadowed by his passing. However, I believe there was another issue with the timing of Taylor's departure. While he never said so, I don't think Taylor was going to allow Jamaal to beat him by finishing a season that he himself couldn't. This wasn't a part-time gig, he once told Jamaal.

I believe it's written in the Bible that a man does not know the hour nor the day his soul will be demanded of him. Taylor did know the time he would depart, and I think he took a certain pleasure knowing that he had 'one up' on the man upstairs. While he kept it all in perspective, Taylor always had to be in control to some extent. He lived and died under his own terms. His wasn't a natural passing, you see. That wasn't part of his plan. He wouldn't have it any other way. He passed the way he lived, and he was in control until the end, at least he thought so.

Afterwards, we were all in a state of shock having just witnessed Taylor's passing. We spent some time together after Taylor's body was taken to the morgue, but not a lot of time. We all wanted to embrace our memories of him, and we wanted to be there for Kaylee, but it was as if a feeling came over all of us at once that demanded we all retreat to our own corners and individually reflect upon the past, contemplate the present, and prepare for the future. There would be time enough at the funeral to lean on one another. Kaylee bid us good-bye, and withdrew to her room. Justin and I finished cleaning up, then I dropped him off downtown at the hotel. I drove home, and felt as if I was the only one on the road. I remember very little of the trip to be honest.

As I pulled into the driveway, I noticed that the clouds were just beginning to roll in as the sun slipped behind the horizon on this autumn evening. The wind was just beginning to make its presence felt. Rain was due in later that night.

I exited my car and walked into the backyard, for no particular reason, and just stared. Perhaps I just wanted to be in one of the last areas where Taylor and I had enjoyed some good times together, what with the cookouts and all that. Maybe I was just a bit confused and heard the footsteps of the grim reaper as I, practically speaking, was probably down to my last decade or so.

I stared at the grill and determined that it was late enough in the year to consider the outdoor cooking season a wrap, so I wheeled it over to the shed, rolled it inside, then locked the door.

Just before I turned to go in the house, a whirlwind swept through the back yard and nearly cleaned the few remaining leaves from my maple tree. That was all. It was very strange. While I wanted that short burst to mean something more than it did, in my heart I knew that this was merely nature's grim reminder to us that the weather was changing and the growing season had come to an end. I knew that was it, but you never know.

It was on a calm, early November morning, just after sunrise, when Taylor was laid to rest. It was his way; it was his wish. He didn't want to take up everyone's day. Services began early that morning, about the time the hazy sun was licking the tops of the trees, but the beams had not yet fought their way to the ground. The morning's temperature was quite average for that time of year hovering between the upper forties and lower fifties. Most of the men only required a suit coat to stay warm while a few of the women sported heavier dress suits, typical of indoor winter attire. We were heading towards that time of year, you know, so this was as good as any time to drag the heavier attire out of the closet and back into the light of day. The surrounding trees gave the appearance of a colder time of year as they had lost most of their protection, yet a few leaves still bravely clung to the branches.

It is worth noting that the surviving members of Vulture weren't in attendance for the day's service. That was to be expected. You see, when the guys got together in town a few months earlier, they all said their good-byes at that point in time. They wanted to end things on a clean and final note. It was a bittersweet moment for them to say the least.

As stated earlier, Taylor was a planner. He even planned his own passing. He took his last breath in the middle of the week so his funeral could take place on a Saturday. He didn't want to inconvenience anyone.

The cemetery seemed exceptionally quiet that morning, and it should have been, for even though Greenwood Cemetery borders nearby State Route Four, there was little traffic on this Saturday morning. Anyone who was anyone in Hamilton turned out for Taylor's funeral.

Even though it's a well-known no-parking zone along the fence bordering the cemetery, a few media trucks took their place in leading a parade of cars that were lined around the perimeter as far as the eye could see. Those vehicles eventually disappeared down the block as they wove their way into the surrounding neighborhoods. The place was packed, and I would have to guess that a turnout such as this hadn't been seen at the cemetery since the fall of a hometown World War II hero some six decades prior.

The chairs had been placed earlier by the grounds crew, but as the great influx of people continued to file in, some of the attendees volunteered to resume the set-up as long as people continued to arrive. They had to keep wiping the seats off because the morning dew seemed to be quite attracted to the metal-backed vinyl cushions on this morning.

The band was there. No, not the entire marching band, although that idea was kicked around. While most of the members were in attendance as mourners, a group of musicians, I believe many from the volunteer basketball band Taylor recruited, formed a group to play slower songs appropriate for the occasion.

Kaylee arranged to have a minister give a Biblical reading and recite a few prayers suitable for the occasion, but the moment that defined the day occurred when Taylor's life was summed up through the eyes of one of his disciples. Jamaal had requested to read a self-composed piece at the funeral. In his delivery, the tempo of his speech was his of his own design. At times it mimicked a rap, other times it flowed like a traditional poem, but it carried a definite, unique rhythm all its own and a message worth listening to. It wasn't his technique that caught everyone's attention. Rather, it was Jamaal, speaking from his heart and delivering what he learned. You see, he had grown well beyond his years during that fall. Jamaal had indeed grown up. His oration brought tears to those in attendance.

Jamaal stepped to the podium, and I have to admit that I've never seen him look better; sad, but well-groomed and cultured nonetheless. I just wanted to go up to him, throw my arm around him and say, "Son, you've done well."

Jamaal was decked out in a crisp black suit, grey shirt, and he topped off his outfit with a black tie that was infused with shiny silver threads throughout. Perhaps wanting to read more into his apparel than was actually intended, I thought the black and grey represented the mourning we all were going through, and the silver strands in the tie represented a glimmer of hope shining through it all.

Jamaal could have dressed in his traditional urban garb, for that was him, but out of respect for the occasion, he spiffed up. Probably in his heart, he heard Taylor say, "That's good. Aspire to be something better today than you were yesterday. That's not being a sell-out." As he was used to being the center of attention, he calmly cleared his throat, looked towards Taylor's casket, and began.

"Taylor Ross, my man, my rock. Today is not just your day. It is the day we give the lessons we learned from you a place in our hearts, then move on. And so we shall. But first, it's important for you to know that even though you were an only child, you were a brother to all. In the beginning, you constructed barriers around your soul and created an island unto yourself, but you eventually learned to open up and share your spiritual wealth to all who graced your shores before becoming one with the ocean once again. I should be so lucky. The world turns, life continues, and so it is written."

All eyes were on Jamaal.

He continued, "When you were a younger man, you ran, you escaped, and you pounded, pounded, pounded your drums. Yet it was your spiritual fists you pounded onto the thin skin of your soul, trying to break free, break away, and all of the while making your mark in life. But life didn't care, for it was tougher and could outlast the rants of any man. It always had; it always will. You see, what makes life so resilient is that it's ever-changing; it's alive and always will be. Your hands were made of dust, and to dust they shall return. Your soul was hardened by the times, yet you still managed to nurture a soft spot in your heart and allowed it to bloom into a beautiful flower in this desert we call life. Doing so brought a sense of completeness to your existence, and in turn welcomed all to gaze upon it. We experienced you, Taylor Ross, and we recall your words when we watched your heavenly concept become a physical reality. And you're right; in the end, all we can say is, "Wow.""

"You also allowed us to brighten *your* life. Before your time was up on this plane, you taught me to believe in myself, to search out to the end of the rainbow, and beat the drum with a little less vigor, yes, with a little less vigor. While there are those who might think that ran counter to what you preached," he said as he glanced once again towards Taylor's casket, "you told me that to do otherwise would drown out everything else life had to offer." Jamaal looked skyward as he summed up his address. "So give to this child of yours, my Lord, a cradle for his soul, salve for his wounds, and a place within our hearts for his spirit to dwell and direct us in our concert of life."

I don't know if that was the end of Jamaal's speech or not because he began to choke up at the last few words. He was obviously troubled at being in this difficult situation. He was not comfortable showing his vulnerability to others. He was used to being the one in control. He quickly looked right then left, then stepped away from the podium. His speech was fine as it was.

Just as he passed in front of the podium, a white dove descended from the tree tops and landed upon Taylor's casket. Of course, we all want to believe in miracles, so we allowed our imaginations to tell us that this was a symbol from Taylor himself letting us know that he was finally at peace. In reality, I think the bird was actually an ashen-colored city pigeon. It was nice nevertheless, but at the conclusion of its brief visit, the bird raised its tail feathers and deposited a little gift on the casket's lid, then departed. I was off to the side with the other pallbearers, and I saw what just occurred, but since the bird was facing the crowd and was on the downside of the casket's lid, I don't think anyone else saw the bird's grand finale. The brief incident left them believing what they wanted, and nothing more.

If he could have, Taylor, in his own humble way, would have said that the pigeon actually *was* sent by him because he really wasn't worthy of 'dove' status. And the pigeon's final act was symbolic of how life treated Taylor in many ways. But few of us escape the slings and arrows life dishes up to us throughout our time here. In the end, Taylor's money and notoriety didn't save him. The lumps he took throughout life, however, transformed his soul into one that was, despite the obstacles it faced, able to love, help, assist, and teach. To overcome those barriers is a most noble legacy for anyone to leave behind.

And speaking of a legacy, Taylor made sure those who meant the most to him were suitably rewarded. He took care of Kaylee, of course, but I wasn't privy to those details. Just as well; it's none of my business. Taylor willed the remaining share of his royalty checks to the music department of the school. The surviving members of Vulture held a small concert, their first in twenty years, in Taylor's memory. Justin filled in for John on lead guitar, and did a pretty good job. Jerry found a stand-in percussionist for the occasion. That might have bothered a lot of people, but it wouldn't have bothered Taylor. He always used to say that good drummers were like cow pies. "We're spread all around this countryside."

All in all, the band sounded pretty good-a little slower, but only slightly so, yet the harmonies were still there. They made a CD of the session and filmed the get-together for cable TV channel VH1. With some of the proceeds, Vulture set up the Taylor Ross Scholarship Fund for the school. They tried to make sure everyone was taken care of.

As stated earlier, there's no need to be concerned for the one who passes. They will be cared for. It's those that are left behind that I pray for. In this case, most of the prayers have been answered, or at least they have been heard.

Rockwood has changed hands. An executive from Los Angeles purchased the estate a year after Taylor's passing. The man lives there with his wife.

Thanks to Bob Harmon's efforts, Jamaal received a partial scholarship to Purdue University and became a member of the Boilermaker Marching Band; a band known for its Big Bass Drum, one of the largest in the land. It seemed only fitting. He works weekends jamming with a combo at some of the area clubs in the West Lafayette, Indiana area, and seems more satisfied in himself as a person than I ever would have imagined. He's actually taken a shine to jazz and does quite well with it. I'm proud of him.

Bob Harmon finished the year out as the band's director, retired with the proper honor and dignity he so deserved, then passed the baton on to his son, a man he rarely saw eye-to-eye with until that summer he and Taylor mended fences. I guess he knew he had his run, and the time had come to pass the torch to a new generation, to coin a phrase.

Bob did a good job in his final year at the helm. He got many, if not most of his students, music scholarships or grants of one sort or another. Mr. Harmon was humble in taking credit for that, though. He said, "Taylor got them the notice they deserved; I just filled out the paperwork." The following winter, Bob and his wife Donna moved to Sedona, Arizona. I still hear from them on occasion.

Kaylee has a special man in her life, but no immediate plans to make things permanent just yet. As she puts it, when a piece of your soul is forever removed, it takes time for sufficient healing to take place before one can venture back out and rest their head on another's shoulder.

The kite those two enjoyed that spring day in the park still hangs in her garage. It's just gathering dust, but she'll never part with it.

She still has the cactus plant on her living room table as well, and I believe it has another new flower bud. And finally, the room wouldn't be complete without her 'World's Best Teacher' statue still sitting on the mantle above her fireplace.

As for me, well, I've befriended a very nice lady. We've known each other for years in passing, but recently we found a common ground in our life's situations. We're content to keep it light right now, and it's working out to the satisfaction of all involved.

I'm still retired, but if you ask me, I think I'm working harder now than when I was employed. I rejoined my church and now help out those in need. It's made me feel useful once again. Also, this season I rejoined the Hamilton High athletic boosters and helped out with some of the events at the school. It helps keep me young to be involved with the students. And you know, every time I see that band take the field, it takes me back to a time when I discovered that sometimes nature does save its best for last.

It is said that everything one does throughout their life reverberates through eternity. I'm not sure how true that is, for many of the things in Hamilton are as they were. Taylor didn't change everything–just our little corner of it. Come hell or high water, the sweet corn still arrives at the produce stands just in time for the Fourth of July holiday. Whenever I stop by and pick up a few ears, I think of Taylor and how his hunger for a final taste of that hometown treat might have actually contributed to his return home.

The school's marching band is still playing, of course. They're still first-rate, although they're not what they were during that special season. But then again, you can't duplicate that. It was a special time in all of our lives. A spirit such as that seldom comes along, and when it does, it has to come from within. It was indeed a magical year.

Taylor certainly gave his all in whipping them into shape, but nobody expected things to end up the way they did. That's not the point. You see, Taylor's efforts weren't about organizing a great band. It was about getting individuals to think in terms of 'I' and 'we' at the same time. It became his mission to assist people in finding their true selves by motivating them to explore their full potential, one member at a time, so that they could play one note at a time, and eventually have them work in unison to create an entire song for the good of the whole. As fate would have it, in the end it was this ambition that drove Taylor to find *his* true self. That was His plan.

*A Different Drummer* is one of K.D. Richardson's nine published titles. Other works by Mr. Richardson include *Reflections of Pearl Harbor*, *The Reawakening*, and *Destiny's Echo*. A graduate of Miami University (OH), K.D. Richardson has been a writer since 1996, and he is also a sports columnist/photographer for the Venice Cornerstone newspaper in Ohio.

Mr. Richardson maintains a website, www.kdrichardson.com, and appreciates any feedback on this or any of his other works.

www.ingramcontent.com/pod-product-compliance
Lightning Source LLC
LaVergne TN
LVHW050337171225
827974LV00005B/113